Self-published by Gaurav Arora

INDIA

ISBN: 978-93-340-2316-9

First Edition

7 Spiritual Laws of Power

GAURAV ARORA

INDEX

FORWARD

It was Diwali - the Festival of Lights in India. I was walking in a busy mall with my wife when I noticed a stall with a man dressed as a priest. The banner on the stall claimed that astrology could solve any life problem. My curiosity piqued, I approached the man, and he began filling up squares. Within minutes, he was ready to answer any questions about my life. I am a practical person and not easily persuaded, but his predictions were surprisingly accurate. He even predicted the financial challenge I was facing and accurately associated it with certain time events. He also suggested some remedies, which I disagreed with, but it left me wondering if life could really be understood by putting some signs into a few boxes.

This experience left me wondering about life and destiny. It made me question if our lives are already written out for us, predetermined in some way. And it made me ponder the possibility of a system that could accurately predict life's outcomes for so many different people with all their unique life paths and situations. Is it really possible to have such a framework that can account for the complexities of human life across the entire globe?

Meeting an astrologer in India isn't unusual, and this was my third time. Each time, their words closely matched things happening in my life. This got me really thinking about astrology. I've always been deep into spirituality and have had some intense experiences, but astrology? I never really believed in it before. Yet, here I was, seeing these matches in my life and starting to wonder if there was something more to these astrological boxes.

In the months that followed, I found myself deeply engaged with astrology. It felt like the Universe was guiding me, blessing me with insights and a new understanding of life's structure.

Vedic astrology, renowned worldwide, claims to map any life situation onto a piece of paper. At first, I was sceptical how could such a vast array of life experiences and situations possibly fit within the confines of a small, nine-inch square? But as I delved deeper, I was amazed. The depth and richness of this ancient framework were staggering. It revealed insights so unique and profound they often left me speechless.

Being an entrepreneur is a journey full of ups and downs, and navigating its challenges is no small feat. This astrological framework became a beacon for me, guiding me through even the darkest times. In this book, I'm sharing this framework as I've come to understand and experience it. It's a collection of my personal insights and learnings. I don't claim to be a spiritual guru, nor am I here to challenge the experts in this field. My aim is to offer what I've discovered on my journey, hoping it might illuminate the path for others as well.

The sole purpose of this book is to empower its readers. If it helps you face life's challenges with more strength and confidence, then it has fulfilled its goal. I hope that through these pages, you'll find the tools and insights to navigate life's journey with a renewed sense of power and clarity.This book isn't about debating the existence of planets within us or questioning how celestial bodies far away might influence our daily lives. It's not concerned with why these cosmic entities would be interested in our affairs. Instead, the heart of this book delves into a more pressing matter: the reality that we, as emotional beings, are often affected by the situations and people around us. It's all too human to feel overpowered by life's various challenges. The essence of this book is to explore these situations and to deeply reflect on what it takes to confront and overcome them with strength and resilience.

This book isn't about presenting spiritual practices, quick fixes, or workarounds. Its purpose is to use the principles of astrology as a tool to gain a deeper understanding of life. With this understanding, you can approach life's challenges with greater strength and control. Knowledge is power – the more you understand something, the more influence you have over it. You won't find traditional astrological rituals, remedies here, or any shortcuts to life's complex questions. Instead, this book is grounded in the foundational principles of astrology, offering insights that empower you to navigate life's forces more effectively.

I present this book with the sincere hope that it will be a source of empowerment. If, in the course of sharing my insights and experiences, I inadvertently contradict anyone's beliefs, understanding, or knowledge on the subject, I offer my apologies. This work is an expression of my journey and is shared with the intention of contributing to a broader conversation about dealing with life more powerfully using the principles of Vedic astrology.

The Power Framework - Introduction

In this chapter, let me introduce you to a unique framework that raises essential questions about the essence of our existence as human beings. It's crucial to recognize that the way you are isn't a chance or a coincidence – it's a part of a grand design, a 'Matrix' into which you were born. Understanding that you are a piece of this Matrix is the first step towards transcending its limitations. This book begins with the intention of helping you grasp the nature of this Matrix, enabling you to navigate your daily life with greater awareness and empowerment.

This framework is not just a tool; it's a comprehensive map of all the emotions that shape your world. My goal here is to distill the essence of power from each element of this framework and present it to you in a clear, distinct manner. This way, you can harness this knowledge to achieve more impactful and meaningful results in your life. While this might seem daunting at first, rest assured that we'll take this journey gradually, building our understanding step by step.

Acknowledgments

First and foremost, I extend my deepest gratitude to the universe for its guidance and inspiration in writing this book. The insights I received were instrumental in bringing these pages to life.

I am profoundly grateful to my wife, Isha, and my family, whose unwavering support was the backbone of this endeavor. Their encouragement and belief in my vision were indispensable.

Lastly, I offer my heartfelt thanks to my daughter, Myrah. Her boundless and selfless love has been a source of endless joy and motivation. This book is not just a product of my efforts but a testament to the love and support of these remarkable individuals.

Last but not the least, a big humble bow down to all my coaches for being a source of power and the selfless contribution to my life.

The easiest and toughest way to be in power is to be in alignment to its nature.

Preface

At the core of our universe lie two fundamental elements: matter and space, both intricately woven with energy. As human beings, we are equipped with senses that enable us to perceive and measure matter. However, the realms of space and energy remain subjects of intense debate, open to various interpretations, perspectives, and beliefs. In recent years, we've made significant strides in understanding how energy influences us daily, yet we recognize that there's still much to explore and comprehend. This journey into a deeper understanding of energy and its impact is where this book begins.

Energy is all-encompassing and ever-transforming, constantly shifting from one form to another. Consider how you might feel energized one day as if you're on top of the world; the next day, you might feel the opposite. This fluctuation leads us to an essential question: Is there an underlying order to how this energy is organized, and can we understand its impact on us? This inquiry is particularly significant as it directly influences our ability to carry out our daily activities and harness our personal power.

Vedic astrology stands as a potent science in understanding life, its relationship with the environment, and its connection to life's events. It intricately weaves together the composition of human energy with the matter surrounding us in space. The widespread belief in Vedic astrology, bolstered by its accuracy and its benefits to many, attests to its power. It's said that the ancient sages who penned these texts received their knowledge directly from the divine. How else could they have accurately described phenomena such as the time for light to travel from the sun to the earth or the orbits of planets around the sun – mysteries that modern science unraveled only after centuries?

There must be some foundational science and a source behind this vast pool of knowledge. It's difficult to dismiss it as mere fiction, especially when it offers insights that can empower us in our daily lives. The relevance of Vedic astrology lies in its ability to provide us with information that can be harnessed for personal empowerment.

The first section of this book is dedicated to establishing a solid foundation in astrology. No prior knowledge of astrology is necessary; the only prerequisite is an open mind. We'll delve into the intricacies of energy and its patterns, identifying where power resides and learning how to tap into it for our personal growth.

I assure you that by following along with this book, you'll gain valuable insights into areas of your life where you may feel powerless. Applying these insights can lead to significant breakthroughs. This journey isn't just about learning; it's about transforming your understanding and leveraging the rich knowledge that this ancient science offers.

So, let's commence this journey - ready to unlock and utilize the immense wisdom that astrology holds for us.

Power is akin to nourishment for the body; it's essential for our daily endeavours and vital for effectively handling the tasks at hand. Regardless of where you stand in life, ascending to the next level invariably requires power. It's not solely about the skills one possesses; the real game-changer is how powerfully a person can apply these skills. This interplay of skill and power is what truly drives transformation and progress.

Power, though intangible, is profoundly felt in our lives. It's elusive, something you can't quite pinpoint, yet its impact on us is undeniable. In our everyday interactions, we constantly gain and lose power due to various situations and people, often without fully understanding why. Have you ever wondered why we let certain things overpower us? Do we truly grasp what causes us to lose our power? It seems that everything is so entangled and occurs beyond our conscious awareness, making it challenging to identify where and how our power slips away. Why do we sometimes lack the reason, energy, or even the desire to pursue what matters most to us?

Is there an underlying reason or structure to the events that unfold in our lives? If we could discern some semblance of order and meaning in the world around us, it would empower us to handle life's challenges more effectively. Recognizing patterns and structures not only provides us with clarity but also equips us with the tools to navigate our experiences with confidence and strength.

The framework of astrology, crafted thousands of years ago by an advanced civilization, is a testament to their profound understanding of the cosmos. This civilization could detail the speed of light, measure the distance between the sun and earth, and even grasp concepts like gravity and centripetal force, all without the modern gadgets and telescopes we rely on today. Astrology, as a spiritual science, offers precise insights at both the human and existential levels. Given its enduring relevance and accuracy, it stands out as a remarkably effective tool for addressing the everyday challenges and questions we face in our lives.

Before we delve into the aspects of the Vedic astrology framework and align it with the power framework, allow me to outline the broader knowledge base of astrological science. We'll explore its structure, dimensions, and mechanics. This foundational understanding will clarify the operation of the framework and enable us to appreciate its intricacies. It will also equip us to apply its wisdom effectively in our pursuit of personal empowerment.

The Power Framework

Before diving into the laws of Power, it's essential to first outline the framework within which these laws operate. Imagine a framework capable of encompassing all life situations of every living being that has ever existed on this planet. The mere thought of constructing such a comprehensive system might overwhelm even the most seasoned management expert. However, by the time you finish this book, you will be convinced, to a significant degree, of the framework's ability to thoroughly encompass and interpret the myriad of life situations we encounter.

I don't ask you to take my word for it blindly; instead, I invite you to test and validate these concepts against your own life experiences as we progress. As you journey through this book, compare its insights with your personal situations and understandings. The basic ground rules will be laid out later, but for now, I have a simple request: temporarily set aside your existing logic, understanding, and beliefs. This approach will provide the necessary space for me to guide you effectively and help you discover something fresh and transformative from this ancient framework.

This book has the potential to be a catalyst for transformation. However, for its insights to fully resonate, there's one thing you need to provide: space. Space that is fresh and free from your existing understanding of life. A space that is fertile and ready to be cultivated.

Setting aside your existing beliefs, even momentarily, creates room for new ideas and perspectives to take root. I demand this space from you, hoping it will facilitate a profound change. My intention is for this book to not just inform you but to transform you. With this request in mind, let's now proceed to explore and understand the framework together.

At the heart of any framework are its components, their interrelations, and their connections with the surrounding environment. This framework follows the same principle. Fundamentally, it's about understanding each individual and their relationships with various situations and people. I'll break down these concepts even further to delve deeper and provide more insightful control over these dynamics. While astrology offers a multitude of layers for comprehension, I'll start with the basics to keep it accessible for beginners. This approach will ensure a solid foundation before we explore this fascinating science's more complex aspects.

This framework focuses on three critical components: 'You,' 'People/Situations,' and 'Your Reactions/Feelings.' Our journey begins with a deep dive into 'You' – unravelling the layers of your personality and understanding what makes you unique. Once we grasp this, we'll expand our view to include 'People/Situations' – exploring how these external factors interact with and influence your life. Finally, we'll examine 'Your Reactions/Feelings' – understanding how these interactions evoke specific emotions and responses. By dissecting these components, we'll gain a comprehensive view of the intricate web of your personal universe.

Breaking You Down into Your Essence

Before delving into the analysis of your physical and psychological makeup, let's pause to understand why this dissection is crucial.

To truly comprehend and master anything, breaking it into its constituent parts is essential. Take a car, for instance: viewed as a whole, it's simply a vehicle. However, to understand how a car operates, you must familiarize yourself with its systems — like the engine, suspension, etc. While you experience the car as a single, composite entity, dissecting these components lets you grasp how they function together. This detailed understanding enables you to troubleshoot and resolve issues more effectively as you gain a deeper insight into each component's role and interplay with others. Similarly, dissecting the aspects of 'You' – your physical traits, mental processes, and emotional patterns – will provide a profound understanding of how you function as a whole.

Just as the primary function of a car is to transport you swiftly to your destination, understanding its mechanics gives you better control and performance, particularly in times of a break down. We value the car's accelerator for the speed it provides, but equally important are the brakes, which, though they slow us down, are crucial for maintaining control. Life's experiences mirror this duality: positive experiences propel us toward our goals, while negative ones, though they may seem to hinder us, are vital for balance and growth. The interplay of positive and negative experiences shapes our journey and our development.

In any machinery, from batteries to complex systems, the coexistence of positive and negative forces is essential for movement and functionality. Humans are no different – we require a balance of positive and negative energies to function optimally.

At this point, redefining and reconsidering our understanding of and relationship with negativity is crucial. Often, negativity is viewed so unfavourably that we instinctively avoid it. However, acknowledging and embracing negativity as an integral part of life is critical. Just as you need to hold a glass to drink water, you need to recognize, acknowledge, and own your negativity to deal with it effectively. This understanding will enable us to explore the coexistence of negativity and positivity within ourselves. We'll identify what is negative and positive in nature and learn to navigate these aspects appropriately.

Let me now switch gears and talk more about the composition pattern of humans. Food is a mixture of many spices and flavours, but it can be summed as good or sour taste to the inexperienced. It only takes an expert to hold the taste in the tongue and know what all comes together to bring that flavour out. Likewise, to fully experience and appreciate life, we need to dissect and understand its various 'flavours' individually. Your body and personality, though functioning as a unified entity, can be broken down for a more profound understanding. In Vedic astrology, this dissection is represented through nine components known as 'Planets.' These include the Sun, Moon, Mercury, Venus, Mars, Jupiter, Saturn, Rahu, and Ketu. While these names might evoke images of celestial bodies in outer space, Vedic astrology teaches us that every entity in existence, from the smallest blade of grass to the vastness of the cosmos, embodies these nine aspects.

So, when I speak of these 'Planets,' I'm referring to the aspects within you that correspond to these celestial entities. We'll use the same terminology as the ancient sages who identified and named these forces millions of years ago. This approach isn't just about tradition; it's about connecting with a time-tested wisdom that views the universe and ourselves as reflections of the same fundamental principles.

This concept might initially sound unusual, even illogical, but I encourage you to stay open-minded and trust the process. As we progress, the pieces will start to fit together, and the framework will become clearer.

Just as every component in a car has a specific function – brakes to halt, suspension to support, the engine to power – each celestial 'planet' in Vedic astrology has a distinct role or 'office' to manage in the grand scheme of life. Let's begin by examining the roles they play and the attributes they possess. Understanding the characteristics and innate nature of these players will gradually unveil how the various elements of life interconnect and function together. This insight is critical to grasping the broader workings of life as depicted in this ancient and profound system.

As we delve further into this journey, I invite you to begin dissecting and examining your own life - its emotions and behaviours. Consider viewing your life through this new lens, where each emotion and reaction is distinctive, offering unique insights. Additionally, I'll be discussing the 'charge' of each planet, whether positive or negative and how these energies influence our experiences.

This approach will deepen your understanding of the astrological framework and provide a fresh perspective on your personal experiences and emotional landscape. By doing so, we will uncover how these celestial forces shape our daily lives and contribute to our overall well-being and personal growth.

Transitioning from a profound exploration of our intrinsic nature and the dynamic interplay of positivity and negativity within us, we now turn our focus towards the influences that these planets have that mould our essence and guide our journey through life. Let's explore how each planet, from Saturn to Mercury, holds keys to unlocking aspects of our character, challenges, and potentials.

Saturn – The Guardian of Karma

Let's begin with one of the most influential aspects of your personality, represented by Saturn. This planet functions like a cosmic overseer, ensuring that you align with the grander laws of nature and maintain good conduct. Saturn is the embodiment of Karma in your life. It operates on a simple yet profound principle: rewarding good deeds and imposing consequences in accordance with universal laws. In this realm, there are no exceptions or shortcuts; the rules are unyielding. Saturn's role is to instil discipline, acting as a stern but fair guide.

While it may be tempting to view Saturn's role negatively due to its strict nature, it's important to recognize its fundamental contribution to building a strong foundation in your life. This aspect is essential in developing your inner strength and resilience, playing a crucial role in your journey towards empowerment. Therefore, understanding and respecting Saturn's influence is of paramount importance, especially in discussions about power. Saturn shoulders a tough but necessary responsibility.

Physically, Saturn is associated with the part of your body extending beyond the pelvis – primarily your thighs and knees.

These areas provide the strength to stand, walk, and run, symbolizing your ability to move forward in life. They are foundational not just in a physical sense, but also in how powerfully and strongly you navigate through life's challenges.

Jupiter - The Catalyst of Expansion

Notably, Jupiter's role as an expansive force is mirrored in its physical manifestation in the cosmos. It's the largest planet in our solar system, more than twice as massive as all the other planets combined. This immense size symbolizes its astrological significance – its unparalleled capacity for growth, expansion, and abundance. Just as it dominates the celestial landscape, so does its influence extend broadly and powerfully in personal growth and creativity.

In the context of power, Jupiter's presence is particularly significant. Its support is essential for fostering new creations and facilitating expansion in various aspects of your life. As we explore the theme of power, understanding and harnessing Jupiter's expansive energy becomes crucial in the journey toward personal development and realizing your creative potential. Additionally, it is situated below the belly region, encompassing the area of your sexual energy, which further underscores its role in creative and generative processes.

Mars: The Driving Force of Action

Mars functions like the engineer of our personal universe, bringing motion and vitality to our internal machinery. Often described as the 'fire in the belly,' the planet fuels and propels us into action, releasing the energy we need to move forward. Mars plays a crucial role in coordinating how all our systems in the machinery – from the nervous to the respiratory – operate seamlessly and efficiently.

This planet is a positive force, if not in excess, constantly pushing us towards progression and action. Its influence is vital in driving movement in our lives, ensuring that we don't just dream and plan but also act and accomplish. Understanding Mars's role can help us tap into our inner strength and motivation, pushing us to overcome inertia and make tangible strides in our personal and professional journeys.

The balance of Mars's energy within us is crucial. An excess of Mars can lead to aggression and impulsiveness. At the same time, a deficiency might result in lethargy or a lack of drive. Physically, Mars governs the belly region of the body, which is often considered the seat of energy and drive. This region's health and vitality reflect Mars's influence on our ability to act and assert ourselves in various aspects of life.

Given the inherent nature of Mars as a driver of action and determination, its role becomes particularly crucial when discussing power.

Venus: The Trap of Comfort and Habit

Venus represents a crucial aspect of your nature: your habits, routines, and the ways you find comfort in life. It is the planet that brings ease and luxury, embodying the very essence of your comfort zone and the familiar patterns you gravitate towards.

While the comforts and habits Venus represents can be enjoyable, they also have a tendency to hold you back, slowing your progress almost imperceptibly. Venus governs not just the comforts but also the addictions and indulgences that can subtly impede growth. It's akin to the fluid and encompassing water element, occupying a significant part of your physical body and nature. Venus's energy is feminine and, in a sense, negative – not in terms of bad or good, but in its capacity to apply brakes to your forward momentum, often in ways you might not immediately recognize.

Consider the fable of the Hare and the Tortoise. Like the hare, we often become complacent and rest on our laurels, especially after achieving a little lead. There's nothing inherently wrong in seeking comfort. Still, it's vital to recognize how staying in the comfort zone can sometimes be disempowering.

Physically, Venus is associated with the heart area, the centre of emotions. Its influence here underscores the emotional dimensions of our comfort and habits, making it a key player in both personal contentment and emotional inertia and its impact on our power.

Mercury: The Realm of Realities

Mercury represents the unvarnished truths of life, existing in the realm of objective facts devoid of emotion. It's the planet of tangible realities – like the figures in your bank statement or the square footage of your house, which stand without room for subjective interpretation. These undeniable numbers define aspects of your existence, offering clarity without ambiguity.

Additionally, Mercury governs your communication – the words you choose not only reflect your current inner state but also how powerfully you are dealing with your life. Language and communication are crucial aspects under Mercury's domain, determining how you connect with the world and express your reality.

Physically, Mercury is associated with the area around your neck and face, particularly your skin. This represents the outward manifestation of your inner state, the 'face' you show to the world. In essence, Mercury is neutral, neither positive nor negative, as it aims to transcend the duality of perception. Reality, as Mercury presents it, is uncoloured by these subjective labels.

In the celestial sphere, Mercury is akin to a solid iron core – a symbol of the fundamental and unembellished essentials of existence. Astrologically, its proximity to the Sun signifies its alignment with life's stark truths and realities.

Moon: The Mind's Ebb

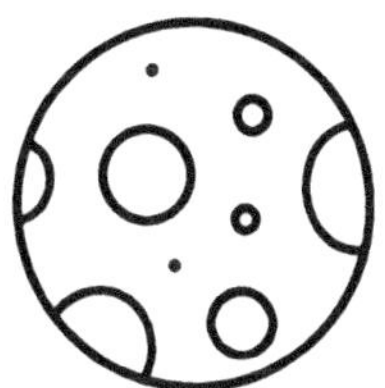

The Moon symbolizes the mind in this astrological framework, acting as the central processing unit and control panel. It interacts with all other planetary components, orchestrating their functions and ensuring everything works harmoniously. It is an inherently social and highly emotional part of our being.

The phases of the Moon add another layer to its significance. With its increasing visibility, the waxing Moon is often associated with positive energy, symbolizing growth and expansion. Conversely, where visibility decreases, the waning Moon represents negative energy, often linked with introspection and decrease. This waxing and waning reflect the natural ebb and flow of life, with the Moon at its core.

The mind, as represented by the Moon, is central to our existence. It is arguably the most critical aspect of our personality, requiring considerable attention and development. Its influence is profound and far-reaching, especially in the context of power. How we harness and manage the power of the mind can significantly impact our journey towards personal empowerment and success.

Sun: The Ultimate Source of Power

The Sun represents the core of your existence – the embodiment of your soul and the quintessence of life itself. In the realm of astrology, the Sun is seen as the primary source of your power and a vital connection to source divine. It illuminates the deepest parts of your being, casting light on your innermost being and spiritual inclinations.

Both the Sun and the Moon are fundamental to your existence, each playing a crucial role in defining who you are. In this book, however, our focus will primarily be on the planets. Understanding the Sun and Moon requires a solid foundational knowledge of astrology – a foundation we aim to build here. Once we have developed a solid understanding and gained some control over the planetary influences, we will have laid the groundwork necessary for delving into the complexities of the Sun and Moon.

Recognizing their profound significance, I plan to dedicate another book to exploring the Sun and Moon. This future work will allow us to explore these celestial bodies in the depth and detail they deserve, building upon the knowledge and insights gained from our current study.

7 Spiritual Laws of Power

Let me sketch out the power framework and start placing the parts on it. I'll keep adding more pieces as we go along.

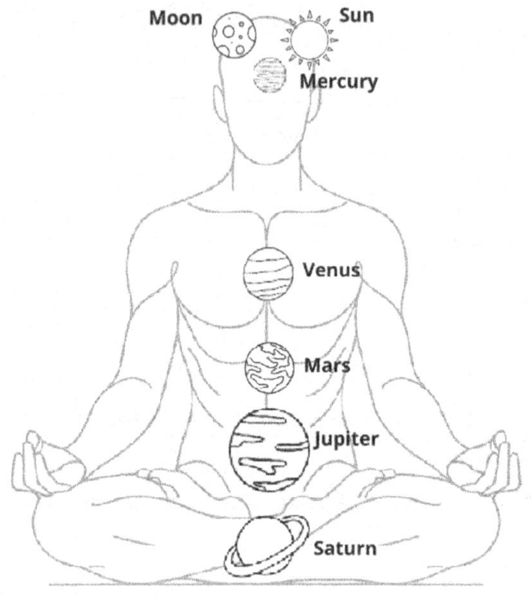

The Power Framework – The Placement of Planets

Rahu and Ketu – The Axis of Growth and Transformation

No exploration of the astrology framework would ever be complete without addressing two pivotal players: Rahu and Ketu. Though they are not physical entities like the other planets but are instead the imaginary north and south nodes, their influence is profoundly real in our lives.

Ketu represents the skills and knowledge that have become second nature to us. It's like learning to drive a car; initially, it requires concentrated effort, but it becomes an automatic process over time. You drive home almost subconsciously, navigating complexities without active thought. Ketu is the accumulation of all that you have mastered – the skills and experiences that are now intrinsic parts of your being, potentially carried over from past lives. Some abilities seem innate, almost like a sense of déjà vu; these fall under Ketu's domain.

Now, let's consider Rahu. Imagine entering an unknown room, peeking in cautiously. This represents your foray into unfamiliar experiences, where everything is new and different. Here, your initial instinct is survival. While physically you might be safe, your mind races with thoughts of adaptation and resilience. You draw on your Ketu – past experiences and skills – to navigate this new environment. This process is where the ego or the egotistical mind comes into play.

Rahu symbolizes this ego mind, always venturing into uncharted territory. It doesn't necessarily signify negative change; sometimes, it can lead to unexpectedly positive developments. However, Rahu is often viewed negatively because of its characteristics of being sudden and uncontrollable. These attributes are typically challenging for us to process. Rahu operates without any set rules and is tasked with the essential role of introducing us to new experiences and lessons.

As you acclimate to this new environment, learning and adapting, the once unfamiliar becomes familiar. What was once a part of Rahu's domain gradually transforms into a part of Ketu – integrated into your being and evolving into second nature.

Both Rahu and Ketu, though negative in nature, are integral to your path of growth. They represent the continuous cycle of encountering the unknown, learning from it, and integrating those lessons into our being, which is the essence of life's journey.

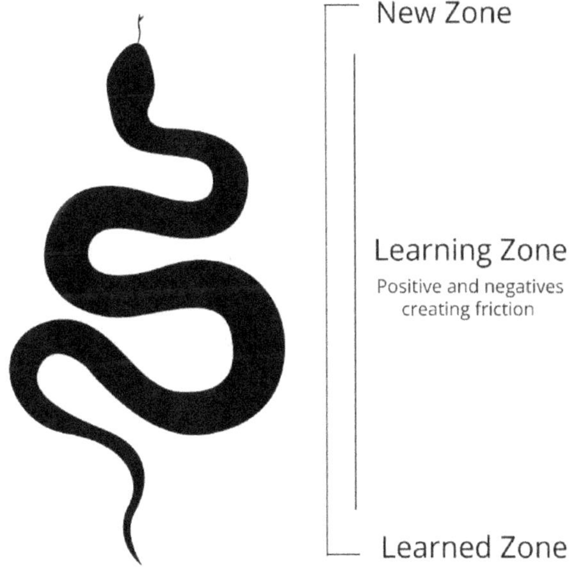

The imagery of a snake is often used to represent the interconnected nature of Rahu and Ketu. In this symbolic representation, Rahu is the head of the snake, while Ketu constitutes the body. This analogy is not just an artistic choice but carries deep spiritual significance.

In many spiritual traditions, the snake is a powerful symbol, often representing wisdom, transformation, and the cycle of life. The snake sheds its skin, symbolizing rebirth and renewal, much like how our experiences and lessons (symbolized by Rahu and Ketu) lead to personal growth and transformation. The head of the snake, Rahu, guides us into new experiences and challenges, while the body, Ketu, carries the wisdom of past experiences. It has now been proved by science that every part of our body has memory.

This representation as a snake beautifully encapsulates the dynamic and cyclical nature of Rahu and Ketu in our lives. They work together in a continuous loop, propelling us forward into new territories (Rahu) and then integrating those experiences into our core being (Ketu), much like the perpetual motion of a snake in motion.

Let me plot Rahu and Ketu on the Power framework chart as well.

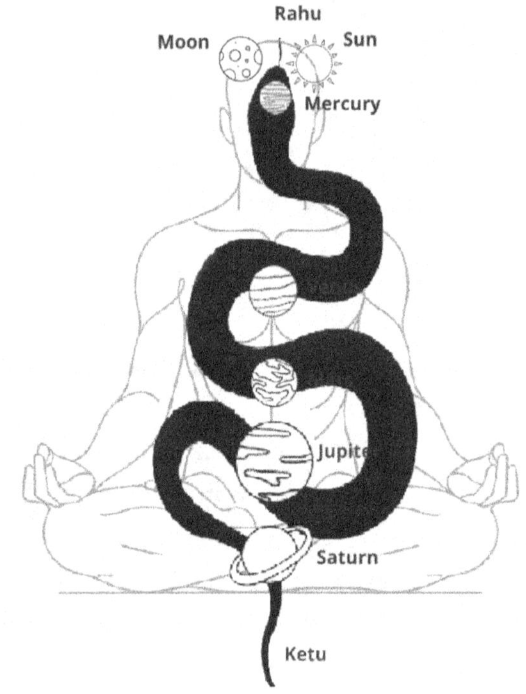

The Power Framework – Planets with Rahu and Ketu

Mastering the Astrological Playing Field

Another way to conceptualize our exploration of this framework is to liken it to a football field, with each planet representing a player on the field. Just as every player has unique strengths and weaknesses, each planet exerts its distinct influence on the game. However, merely knowing the players isn't sufficient. If you aim to engage in the game powerfully, it is equally crucial to understand the field– the broader context in which the players operate.

Furthermore, being aware of the current mood and form of each 'player' during the game – how each planet's influence might be enhanced or diminished under different circumstances – can significantly improve your ability to hold the game together.

Now that we have an overview of the players – the planets – it's time to delve into the 'field conditions.' This involves exploring the environment and contexts in which these planetary influences play out and how they interact with each other within the larger framework of your life.

Culture

Culture or the field we play plays a pivotal role in shaping our personalities. Imagine viewing it from a higher perspective – it encompasses everything we know and experience. Think of yourself as a drop in a river's current. How much control does that single drop have? It's carried by the flow, much like how we are shaped and guided by the cultural currents around us.

I encourage you to reflect on the extent of culture's influence. Consider how your thoughts and perceived options are often a product of the cultural environment you're immersed in. It's crucial to recognize that our immediate surroundings, rather than distant events or people, predominantly shape our perspectives and decisions.

Culture is akin to the water surrounding a fish – it's transparent, life-giving, and so pervasive that it often goes unnoticed. I have witnessed individuals transform simply by changing their social circle or relocating to a different country. Such shifts can profoundly alter one's perspective and identity.

Life, through the lens of our culture, tends to present us with a predefined set of options: our family background, social status, and material possessions. We often spend our lives navigating within these parameters, absorbed in the roles and expectations set by our cultural environment. Remember, you were born into this cultural framework; it existed before you and will continue after. Breaking free from these ingrained patterns requires conscious effort and a deep understanding of the complete framework.

In the upcoming section of the book, we'll focus on gaining an understanding of these internal and external influences. It's about understanding how cultural norms, expectations, and influences – operate within the framework.

Let's start by defining the field, an elliptical ground where the game is played. The field is divided into 12 equal parts, each spanning 30 degrees. These segments, known as the signs or Rashi, each possess their own unique energy and emotional resonance, offering distinct experiences much like varying terrains on Earth. Imagine the difference in emotions evoked by being next to sea shore compared to the feelings when you go to a health club. Each environment elicits its own set of responses.

These 12 arcs are not just arbitrary divisions; they are laden with emotional intent. While emotions may seem random, they follow a system influenced by the energies of these signs. Recall our discussion about culture and its subtle yet profound impact on you, often without your conscious awareness. This cultural influence intertwines with the energies of the signs to shape your experiences and emotions.

We mentioned the differing experiences and emotions evoked by visiting different places - a religious site Vs a health club, for example. Each setting carries a unique energy, impacting you in distinct ways. Similarly, the energies of the signs play a significant role in moulding our personalities and emotional responses.

With this understanding, let's now embark on a sequential exploration of how energy organizes itself within each sign and the specific emotions and thought patterns associated with these astrological segments.

Emotions are a potent force in our lives, impacting us deeply and tangibly. Since they have such a real and powerful effect, it's essential to understand where they reside or originate. Addressing this question is crucial: in what domain do our emotions exist? Without pinpointing their place in the cosmic scheme, gaining a true understanding or control over them remains elusive.

Often, our emotions are entangled and complex, presenting themselves as a composite mix that either empowers or disempowers us. In fact, power itself is an emotion, and its presence can be measured by the effectiveness of the underlying emotions in generating desired results. A powerful emotional state leads to impactful outcomes, whereas a weak one might result in stagnation.

With this in mind, let's proceed sequentially to explore how energy is organized within the astrological framework and how it gives rise to specific emotions. We'll delve into each section of the signs, examining the nature of thoughts and feelings associated with these critical elements and uncovering the emotional terrain that shapes our experiences and actions.

A few days, we are happy, and the next moment, we fear losing this happiness. There is anxiety, love, and courage – so many feelings that live inside us, and they are so real. If they live inside and impact our power, then it is essential to understand them so we can deal with them powerfully. In the power framework, we would point out what emotions exist where and then discuss how we can harness the knowledge of their position and effectively locate the houses of power.

Before we dive deeper, I want to make an important distinction. The following discussion is not about sun signs or zodiacs in the traditional sense, which many of us are familiar with. While related, Vedic astrology serves a different purpose and is interpreted differently. For our discussion, we're focusing on a more specific aspect of signs in the Vedic astrological framework. The emotions in these signs are created to align the energies to maintain an overall cosmic balance and provide a culture that aligns with a bigger purpose.

In astrology, each sign is unique. It's not just a symbol; each one has a unique purpose and meaning. Think of each sign as a key that unlocks a specific emotion or feeling. These signs' pictures or symbols reflect the emotions or situations they are connected to. It's like they're speaking a language of feelings.

In the old ways of Vedic astrology, these signs are also known as 'Rashi'. Every Rashi has its unique energy vibration that can make you feel a certain way. To understand what it's like to feel this energy, think about how you feel when you see the sign associated with the Rashi. This hints at the emotion connected to being in that situation. So, we will look at all the signs one after another and cover the emotion each sign is about.

This will help you understand the link between the sign and what it represents. As we explore each of the astrological signs, it's essential that you connect with the emotions they represent. Remember, every human being has all these emotions inside them. They're just waiting to be noticed or brought into focus.

As we discuss each sign, try to feel and recognize these emotions in yourself. It's like waking them up as we talk about them.

This is similar to an idea in science called 'Quantum Superposition.' It suggests that tiny particles exist in many possible states simultaneously, but they settle into one state when we observe them. In the same way, your attention and engagement with each sign will bring its emotions to life in your own experience. So, let's start this journey with an open mind and see how each sign's emotions show up in us.

7 Spiritual Laws of Power

Let me also include the signs in Power Framework diagram

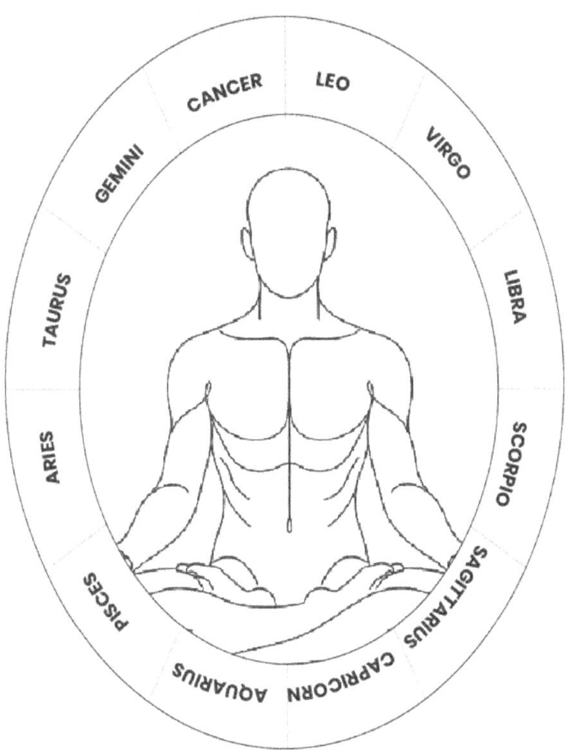

below.

Aries (The Ram): The Ascent to Greater Heights

Aries is symbolized by the Mountain Goat. It has a consistent drive to ascend to higher altitudes. In nature, mountain goats are often seen persistently climbing, solitary in their pursuit of the next peak. The emotions it generates are focused on personal advancement and achievement. This sign embodies a focused, individualistic drive, always striving for greater heights. This symbol of the goat aligns perfectly with the essence of Aries, which encourages the pursuit of personal goals and self-improvement. It's an energy that motivates one to continuously push their boundaries, seeking the next level in their personal and professional lives.

Taurus (The Bull)

Taurus, symbolized by the Bull, represents a phase of energy characterized by a strong instinct towards material acquisition and practicality. This sign is often associated with a certain kind of aggression, but it's not just about raw force. Instead, it's a determined drive to build, create, and possess. Taurus energy is grounded in the tangible and physical aspects of life.

This sign embodies the desire to accumulate material possessions, but it is not solely driven by materialism. Taurus channels its energy into creating and nurturing, whether it is cultivating a garden, building a business, or creating a comfortable home. It's about the practical application of effort to achieve tangible results and the satisfaction derived from these achievements.

Gemini (The Twins): Navigating the Duality of Existence

Gemini, symbolized by The Twins, is all about the concept of duality – how things are defined by their opposites. It helps us understand why we can't have ideas like 'tall' without 'short,' or 'happy' without 'sad.' Everything has its opposite, and that's what gives it meaning.

A lot of what we feel comes from comparing – whether it's comparing ourselves to others or our past selves. We often decide if something is good or bad based on these comparisons. This comparison is duality at work in our emotions. When you start noticing this, you'll see that many of your feelings are tied to this idea of duality – having one thing means understanding or experience related to its opposite.

Cancer (The Crab): The Realm of Social Connectivity

Cancer is represented by the Crab, and to understand Cancer, it's essential to consider the nature of a crab. Crabs are known for their protective shells that safeguard their bodies, much like Cancer, which symbolizes protection and a tendency to be private about personal spaces. Crabs also exhibit social behaviour similar to humans – at times, they are supportive and cooperative with each other, and at other times, they can display aggression.

The range of emotions associated with Cancer is broad and reflects its social aspect. It includes feelings related to protecting oneself and one's home, being sensitive, and experiencing emotional swings that often occur in social settings. The sign of Cancer also encompasses intuition and creativity. These diverse emotions are the result of the complex dynamics found within social interactions. Cancer, therefore, represents a blend of protective instincts, deep sensitivity, and the varied emotional experiences that come from being part of a social community.

Leo (The Lion): The Seat of Power

Leo, symbolized by a Lion, is full of strong and confident emotions. When you think of Leo, think of the proud and brave feeling a lion has. The Leo sign represents the feeling of being powerful. Imagine how it feels to take control and lead - that's what Leo stands for. This sign shows an emotional drive to follow what you're truly meant to do, even though it's not simple. Handling these feelings requires bravery and self-belief to step away from the usual path and pursue your real purpose. This kind of attitude can influence others in different ways: it can motivate and intimidate them, or some might even see this emotional aspect as being too stubborn. However, for someone with Leo's emotional influence, it feels like nothing can stop them.

Virgo : A Sign of simplicity and Care

The sign of Virgo represents the essence of youthful purity and innocence, reminiscent of a young girl who has not yet experienced the complexities of life. It signifies a return to simplicity and the fundamental virtues of practicality and reliability, evoking an unblemished spirit engaging with the world with a light-heartedness and an untainted perspective.

In terms of emotions, Virgo embodies the qualities of staying untouched and unspoiled by life's harsher realities. It symbolizes the strength found in simplicity, the power of a clear, unburdened mind approaching life with freshness and a sense of duty. A meticulous and analytical approach marks the emotional realm of Virgo, coupled with a deep-seated desire to serve others, embodying kindness, sensitivity, and a strong sense of caring for surroundings. Virgo's influence encourages us to face daily life with a smile, unburdened by complexities, embodying the serene strength of youth.

At its core, Virgo is about maintaining purity—not just in a physical sense but in a moral and ethical dimension as you walk through life's challenges. This approach to life, inspired by Virgo, suggests tackling challenges with mental agility, attention to detail, and an earthbound sensibility.

Libra (Scale): Embracing Balance and Harmony

Libra is represented by the scale symbol, which perfectly captures its essence of equilibrium. This sign is about finding balance, fairness, and harmony in every part of life.

The emotions tied to Libra are centred around resolving conflicts and bringing balance not just within oneself but also in the environment. This sign tends to avoid extremes and prefers finding a middle ground in situations to bring balance in life.

The heart of Libra's nature is to establish balance, both in personal life and in the larger cosmic scheme. Libra involves making thoughtful decisions and choices that contribute to and bring back the lost balance in the previous signs' journey. It is the seventh sign and a midpoint that offers an opportunity for reflection emphasizing balance. Decisions made under Libra's influence aim to preserve or re-establish balance, highlighting the significance of thoughtfulness and consideration in shaping one's life.

Scorpio (Scorpio) : Delving into the Mysteries

Scorpio is a sign that's all about the mysteries of life. It's like encountering energies beyond the surface of things and understand the deeper, hidden parts of life. Scorpio is connected to the things we can't see, like secrets or the unknown.

The feelings that come with Scorpio are often about things we don't fully understand. It's like being in a dark room where secrets and mysteries are hidden. Scorpio makes us think about the deeper questions of life – the 'why' and 'how' of things that are not clear or are hidden from view.

Emotions related to Scorpio often involve dealing with the unknown or secret things. It's about trying to make sense of the things that puzzle us or that we don't know much about. Scorpio brings feelings of curiosity, but also a mix of fear or wonder about these mysteries.

Sagittarius : The Archer's Quest

Sagittarius is represented by the Archer, which is depicted as a centaur. This creature is a combination of a human and a horse. The image of the Archer aiming an arrow towards the sky represents what Sagittarius is about.

Sagittarius is a sign that aims to set its eyes on big goals and pursue them with great determination and stability. The Archer's four legs symbolize the most stable and strong position for a human to stand on, which perfectly embodies the emotions in the Sagittarius sign.

Imagine how empowering it could be to find and steadily move towards the goal. That is how it feels to be in the Sagittarius domain.

Capricorn (Makara): The Guardian of Discipline and Endurance

Capricorn is represented by Makara, a legendary sea creature from ancient Vedic times, often depicted as a dragon-like entity. It combines the features of a deer and an amphibian, creating a powerful symbol of strength and mystery. Makara is also known as a guardian of gateways and thresholds, symbolizing protection and vigilance.

In the emotional landscape of Capricorn, Makara's imagery resonates with feelings of discipline, responsibility, and endurance. The image of a red-flying dragon, often associated with fear, can be interpreted as a driving force behind these attributes. This fear isn't about being scared; it's about the respect and caution that motivates hard work and dedication and holds back the non-deserving of passing through.

In my spiritual experience, I can feel the fear generated in this arc of energies just by the mere sight of the Makar, which, in my experience, was a scary flying red dragon, nothing close to anything I have seen.

Capricorn energy encourages holding onto principles. It's about persevering through difficulties and being courageous in facing obstacles. This sign symbolizes the journey of enduring and overcoming.

Aquarius (The Water Bearer): The Neutral Dispenser of Karma

Aquarius is symbolized by the water bearer, holding a pitcher that represents the collective karma. This sign is about serving the contents of this pitcher, reflecting the notion that you reap what you sow. The open pitcher signifies that these karmic accounts are always active and ongoing. Unlike other signs, Aquarius is not deeply associated with any specific emotions. It doesn't judge or differentiate; it simply dispenses what's inside: rewards or consequences.

The imagery of the lone pitcher, impartially pouring out its contents, symbolizes the maturity and wisdom required to serve without discrimination.

In my own spiritual experience, I saw an open pitcher and felt no emotions. At first, it was strange, as I had never experienced any sign without emotions before, but that is how Aquarius is. Aquarius is about doing its duty, which is to distribute the results of actions. This sign brings with it qualities of discipline and structure. The overarching theme is the progression of humanity and the establishment of fairness, symbolized by the equitable distribution of the pitcher's contents.

Pisces (Rotating Fish) : Embracing Closure and Non-Attachment

Pisces, symbolized by the Fish, represents the final phase of the emotional cycle. It deals with the feelings that arise when we bring things to a close. This sign is about feeling our attachments, especially to things, people, or situations that are ending. Pisces is an energy space for us to enquire how deeply we hold to attachments and what it feels like to let go.

In my spiritual experience of Pisces, I witnessed a fish swimming and suddenly encountering a shipwreck. However, without any attachment or hard feelings, the fish promptly turned around and resumed swimming. It was void of any regrets or recourses.

Pisces is all about moving effortlessly, without getting stuck on thoughts or attachments. It's like hitting a wall, then turning back with ease and comfort. This ability to turn and move on without clinging to the past is at the heart of Pisces. Pisces embodies the idea of flowing with life's changes, releasing what's finished, and gracefully embracing new beginnings.

As we conclude our exploration of the twelve signs, it's essential to understand that the arrangement of these energies is far from random. Each of the twelve segments, spanning 30 degrees within the 360-degree astrological circle, is specifically designed to evoke and generate distinct emotions. These signs are not just symbols; they are dynamic forces that shape our experiences and perceptions.

In any creation or aspect of life, the energy flows through this complete circle, touching upon each of these signs and their unique emotional landscapes. This cosmic distribution ensures a balanced and comprehensive range of experiences, from the initiation of Aries to the closure of Pisces and everything we experience along the journey.

This deliberate and intricate arrangement of energies within the playfield of life offers a profound and holistic understanding of human experiences, emotions, and journeys. It's a reminder of the interconnectedness and purposefulness that underlie our existence in this vast and intricate universe.

Astrological Houses: The External Manifestations of Internal Energies

Having explored the planets, which reveal 'what' energy is being expressed, and the signs, which show 'how' this energy is expressed, we now turn to the astrological houses. The houses address 'where' in our lives this energy will manifest. Like the signs, there are twelve houses, each corresponding to a different life area. While the signs are more internal and express themselves through emotions, the houses are external and have a tangible presence in the world. They are measurable and visible, representing life's physical and material aspects.

These houses are essential because they anchor the energies of the planets and signs into specific areas of our existence. They involve people, situations, and material aspects that remind us of particular lessons and needs in our journey. The influences in these houses stay with us as long as they serve a purpose in our lives and evolve as we progress through different stages.

To simply understand, houses are where our internal energies show up in physicality in our lives, or vice versa. You can look at the physical realities in the houses and then match how internal energies are like. This interplay between the internal and external allows a profound understanding of how internal planet alignments and combinations in different signs manifest in our daily lives. By observing the activities and themes of each house, we gain insights into how our internal states—our thoughts, feelings, and spiritual inclinations—are mirrored in the external world.

Now, let's delve into what these houses represent and how they influence the various aspects of our lives. Following the incorporation of the astrological houses, our "Power Framework" diagram has been updated to include this external dimension.

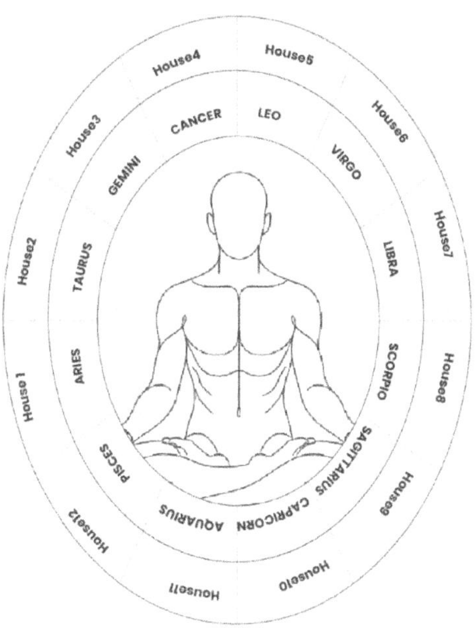

First House: The Self Represents you as a person – your physical appearance, attributes, and overall personality.

Second House: Wealth and Possessions - Focuses on your wealth, assets, material possessions, and financial resources.

Third House: Siblings and Communication - Covers your relationships with siblings and neighbours and your ability to think critically, analyze information and communicate.

Fourth House: Home and Family - This is the house of your home, family, mother, country, and properties.

Fifth House: Creation and Children - Represents the physical things you've created, including your children and creative efforts.

Sixth House: Challenges - Deals with debts, enemies, diseases, and competition – generally the aspects of life you might find challenging or unpleasant.

Seventh House: Partnerships Focuses on your spouse, business partnerships, and close relationships.

Eighth House: Mysteries and Secrets - This is the house of secrets and mysterious life happenings that defy your logical understanding.

Ninth House: Growth and Guidance - Includes your mentors, gurus, and those who contribute to your personal and spiritual growth.

Tenth House: Career and Effort This house is about your career, job, professional life, and the effort you put into your work.

Eleventh House: Gains and Desires Focuses on your income, gains, and fulfilling your desires.

Twelfth House: Endings and Loss Represents losses, unhappy endings, and the departure of things and people from your life. It also encompasses the concept of death.

Integrating Houses, Signs, and Ascendant: A Simplified View

Understanding the complexities of astrology can be challenging and I committed to simplify it. As we discussed, our emotions are greatly influenced by our culture – the way our environment shapes us and, in turn, how we shape our environment based on our feelings. Now, let's see how this tie into the arrangement of energies in the 12 houses, each spanning again 30 degrees.

Imagine signs as a circular train track with 12 stations, each representing a sign. The journey can begin at any of these stations. The sign on the eastern horizon at the time and place of your birth is like the station where you first get on the train – that sign becomes your first house or the Ascendant. It may be the seventh station (sign) on the train's route, but for you, it's where your journey begins, so it is your first house.

If it was the perfect world, your first house and first sign - Aries would be one, but that's rarely the case. Suppose your journey starts with Taurus. Then Taurus becomes your first house, and your personality is influenced by Taurus's nature, which focuses on acquiring physical possessions and stability.

From there, you lay out the rest of your houses sequentially, following the order of the signs. Each house will interact with the energies of its corresponding sign, creating a unique framework that shapes your life's path and experiences. This way, the entire sign wheel becomes a personalized map of your journey, reflecting your emotional, physical, and spiritual growth.

Bringing It All Together: Planets, Signs, and Houses in Astrology

Now that we know about the three essential parts of astrology – planets, signs, and houses – that's all we need. With these, we can create a complete picture. Let's see how they all work together.

Picking back the example of the football field, where the planets are the players in the game. These players (planets) are not just moving around aimlessly; they are influenced by their emotions (signs) and the different areas of the field they find themselves in (houses). Like a football player, each planet has a preferred position where it performs best. However, during the game, they keep moving, adapting to various spots on the field.

At times, a planet might be in a strong, favourable position, perfectly aligned with its nature. But at other times, it might be in a spot that's new or challenging. Each planet's unique characteristics significantly affect how the game unfolds. Their positioning on the field – in different signs – can dramatically impact the game's dynamics.

Let's set up our astrological 'football field' to see how all the pieces (planets, signs, and houses) come together and interact in the game called life.

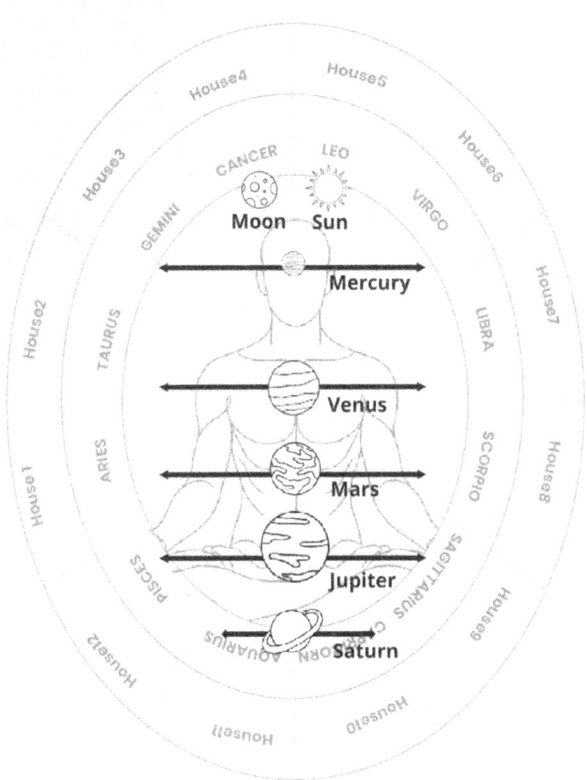

We'll arrange the three elements (Planets, Signs, and Houses) in their perfect spots from the start so the game can unfold in the strongest way possible. The field is in prime condition, and each player is at their most powerful spot. This setup is the best and highest-performing arrangement of our framework.

Saturn finds its greatest strength in the signs of Capricorn and Aquarius. In these positions, it aligns naturally with its core functions and flourishes in its role. In Capricorn, Saturn harnesses the emotion of fear to drive discipline and hard work. It's about setting high standards, pushing for achievements, and using fear as a motivator to get things done efficiently.

Moving to Aquarius, Saturn shifts its approach to maintaining moral accounts through the philosophy of reward and punishment. This placement allows Saturn to oversee and balance on the scales of right and wrong, fairness, and justice. It's a position where Saturn can effectively keep track of moral actions and reactions.

In both these signs, Saturn is in its strongest position. The emotions and energies of Capricorn and Aquarius are perfectly aligned with Saturn's nature. It's like going to a workplace where everything feels right, and you're naturally motivated to do your best. Saturn, in these signs, is empowered to fulfil its duties, demonstrating the importance of alignment in the power framework.

Jupiter, known for its expansive nature, finds its most favourable positions in the signs of Pisces and Sagittarius. These placements align perfectly with Jupiter's core characteristic of expansion.

In Sagittarius, Jupiter thrives on emotions that inspire growth and development by setting new goals and being focused. This sign fuels the desire to learn and broaden one's horizons. Sagittarius provides the perfect emotional environment for Jupiter to encourage personal and spiritual growth.

Pisces, on the other hand, offers a unique advantage to Jupiter's expansionist tendencies. In Pisces, Jupiter operates in an atmosphere where attachment is minimized, keeping the pathways to expansion open and fluid. This sign supports Jupiter's nature by allowing growth and expansion without being held back by emotional ties or restrictions. Pisces creates a space where Jupiter can work its magic of enlargement and enrichment without constraints, making it an ideal position for Jupiter to express its true essence.

Mars, the planet known for its assertiveness and action, finds its greatest strengths in the signs of Aries and Scorpio. Each of these signs uniquely complements Mars, enhancing its dynamic qualities.

In Aries, Mars is in its element. Aries is characterized by a constant drive for action and moving to the next level, which resonates deeply with Mars' love for activity and progress. The emotions associated with Aries – such as enthusiasm, courage, and a pioneering spirit – are incredibly conducive to Mars' energetic nature. This sign creates an environment where Mars can stimulate significant action and drive.

On the other hand, Scorpio adds a different dimension to Mars' strength. While Aries fuels Mars with the energy for action, Scorpio's mysterious and concealed nature keeps the results of actions unpredictable. This uncertainty is crucial because the anticipation of unknown outcomes can maintain a high level of motivation and prevent complacency. It is undoubtedly the other way around as well; the unpredictability of results often deters action. It's believed that Scorpio is where your karmic balances are connected to the source for accounting purposes. In Scorpio, Mars operates in an atmosphere where the end results are not immediately visible. Maintaining strong and persistent drive for action is key, and this hidden aspect of Scorpio ensures the balance of Mars' energies in action.

Venus finds its ruling signs in Taurus and Libra due to its affinity for leisure, comfort, and individuality. These signs provide environments that resonate deeply with Venus' nature, each in their unique way.

In Taurus, Venus is right at home. Taurus is about the love of comfort and the desire for material possessions and assets. This sign creates a nurturing environment where Venus' qualities of appreciating beauty and comfort are amplified. The energies of Taurus encourage Venus to indulge in its desires for a luxurious and leisurely lifestyle, making it an ideal setting for Venus to express itself fully.

On the other hand, Libra brings out a different aspect of Venus. Libra is about making choices and decisions, often focusing on maintaining balance and harmony. Since our decisions are primarily based on past experiences and a preference for minimal risk, Venus finds comfort in Libra's tendency towards safe and familiar choices. This sign supports Venus' inclination to stay within the comfort zone, ensuring a harmonious and comfortable loop of decision-making and preferences.

Together, Taurus and Libra create the perfect environments for Venus to thrive, aligning with its love for beauty, comfort, and ease and its tendency to seek balance and harmony in choices and relationships.

It is essential to appreciate Venus, Taurus, and Libra for their positive contribution to life. Venus represents life and beauty, embodying what makes life worth living. While the domain of Venus may not always be associated with traditional notions of power, it is indispensable for its role in sustaining life and adding beauty to our existence. Life without Venus' influence would lack the joy and pleasure that make the journey enjoyable.

Moving to Mercury, which is associated with practicality and intellect, finds its most favourable placements in Gemini and Virgo. These signs align well with Mercury's nature, allowing it to express and operate effectively.

In Gemini, Mercury thrives on expression through language and communication. Mercury is the result, and what we speak is a combination of all emotions. At the same time, what we do is also the sum total of all our experiences.

Gemini, a sign of duality and intellect, provides Mercury with a dynamic and versatile platform. This sign enhances Mercury's ability to communicate effectively, engage in intellectual pursuits, and adapt to various forms of expression. It perfectly matches Mercury's love for exchanging ideas and information, making Gemini an ideal setting for this planet to manifest its communicative strengths.

Virgo, on the other hand, allows Mercury to deal with the practical realities of life. Mercury's practical side is highlighted in Virgo, focusing on details, analysis, and systematic thinking. This sign complements Mercury's logical and analytical tendencies, enabling it to express its true nature through practical solutions and efficient organization.

Gemini and Virgo provide Mercury with the perfect environments to showcase its intellectual, communicative, and practical abilities. These signs allow Mercury to express itself fully, whether through the science of communication in Gemini or the practical application of life skills in Virgo.

The Moon and Sun, two critical aspects in astrology, find their most harmonious placements in Cancer and Leo, respectively.

The Moon, associated with emotions and social instincts, performs exceptionally well in Cancer. This sign, symbolized by the nurturing and protective Crab, aligns perfectly with the Moon's qualities. In Cancer, the Moon gets the opportunity to fully express its social nature, tapping into deep emotional instincts. This placement allows the Moon to thrive in a familiar and comfortable environment.

The Sun, representing vitality and self-expression, naturally excels in Leo. Leo, symbolized by the regal Lion, resonates with the Sun's brightness, confidence, and leadership qualities. In Leo, the Sun finds a suitable stage to shine at its brightest, showcasing its strength and radiance.

While there is much more to discuss about the Moon in Cancer and the Sun in Leo, we'll keep it brief for the scope of this book, acknowledging their ideal placements in these signs.

To stay committed to keeping things easy to understand, I would take an opportunity to tweak the "Power Framework" visual diagram to help you understand more easily. It's made more vertical than spherical to give you a clearer picture of how the astrological system works. However, it's essential to remember that each sign is still a 30-degree arch in the sign circle; it is just a representational change for better understanding.

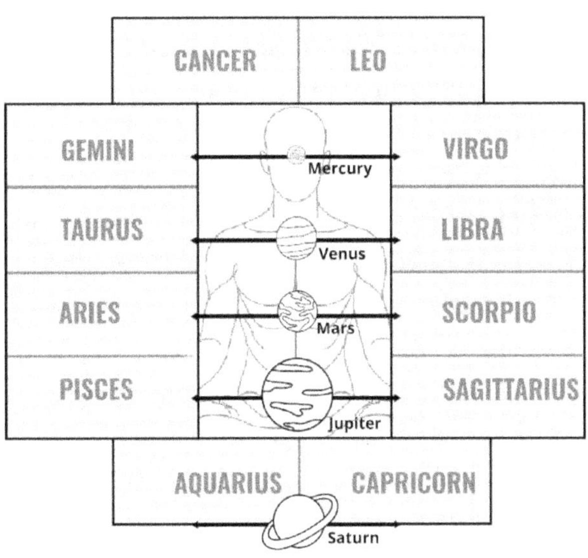

The Game of Power

During a visit to a science fair with my 8-year-old daughter, we stumbled upon a fascinating exhibit about electrical circuits. As she engaged with the displays, her curiosity and excitement were palpable. Amid the bustling fair, a simple yet profound statement caught my attention: 'You can only generate power when both negative and positive charge come together.'

This line resonated with me deeply, not just in the context of science but as a metaphor for life and, interestingly, for astrology. It reminded me of the intricate balance in the universe, where contrasting forces coexist and interact to create energy and movement.

For instance, consider Capricorn, which is often associated with fear and restraint. These qualities might be seen as negative because they can hold people back. However, this 'negative' nature is crucial as it creates a necessary tension or challenge that can lead to growth and stability. Similarly, Aquarius, driven by the 'positive' motivation of reward and progress, propels people forward, creating movement and change.

The notion of negativity in astrology shouldn't be misconstrued as inherently bad. It's an essential counterbalance to positivity. Attachments, represented by signs like Pisces, might be seen as negative due to their restricted nature. At the same time, the unknown, a prominent feature of Scorpio, also falls into the negative category due to its capacity to make things unclear and obscure.

Just as negative charges are essential in providing resistance and balance to positive forces in electrical circuits, the same principle applies in astrology. These 'negative' energies are not detrimental but necessary to create a dynamic equilibrium. They challenge us, prompting growth and development.

Think of it in terms of driving a car. If you understand the mechanics of your vehicle and the terrain you're navigating, you can confidently accelerate, knowing when to speed up and when to apply the brakes. This is important for maintaining tight control of the car and the very essence of power. Life requires a balance of acceleration and restraint. The key is understanding. With a deeper comprehension of how various aspects of your life work together, you gain more control, enabling you to move forward with greater confidence and power.

Let us further look at the negative areas by definition of astrology and have the potential to diminish the power of the planets in our astrological charts. By becoming aware of these factors, we consciously make choices that minimize the impact of negative energies. This awareness would allow us to unlock new power in areas where it was previously lacking. It would provide us with an opportunity to actively participate in life rather than passively experiencing it.

Aries, Gemini, Leo, Libra, Sagittarius, and Aquarius are described as having a positive energy. On the other hand, Taurus, Cancer, Virgo, Scorpio, Capricorn, and Pisces have a negative energy.

It's important to remember that I'm not talking about the usual traits or features of the zodiac signs commonly used in Astrology. That's a whole different subject with its own set of rules.

Let's proceed to explore how we can mitigate the influence of negative energies and boost the planets' strengths, thereby empowering ourselves in the process.

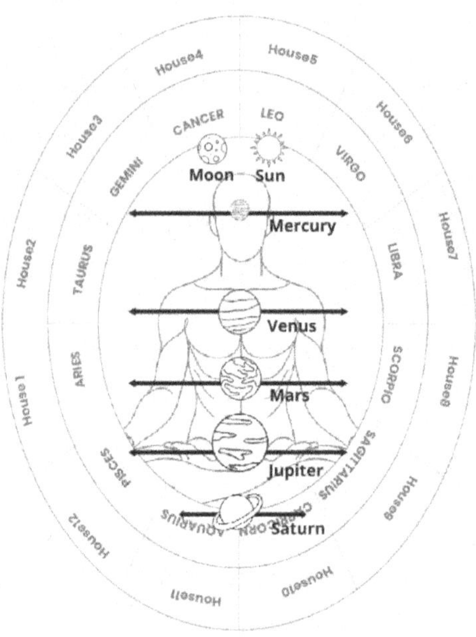

Let's me add two behavioral concepts to experience the energies of the field a level deeper: Elements and Modality.

These are part of your natural makeup, so they should be easy to grasp.

Nature comprises five essential elements: Fire, Earth, Air, Water, and Space. Space is the vastness where everything exists, but we'll focus on the four elements related to the signs. Aries, Leo, and Sagittarius are grouped under Fire signs; they often show fire-like qualities like boldness and warmth. Taurus, Virgo, and Capricorn are Earth signs, reflecting the grounded, stable, and practical aspects of the Earth. Gemini, Libra, and Aquarius fall under Air signs and possess qualities reminiscent of the element of air itself: invisible, essential, and all-encompassing, like communication and relationships. Lastly, Water signs Cancer, Scorpio, and Pisces resonate with Water's fluid, intuitive, and emotional nature.

Moving to modality, it relates to how the signs behave. Cardinal signs are the ones that kick things off and start new projects. Fixed signs are usually set in their ways and don't change much. Mutable signs are flexible; they prepare for what's coming next and are linked with endings.

The Cardinal signs are Aries, Cancer, Libra, and Capricorn. The Fixed signs include Taurus, Leo, Scorpio, and Aquarius. The Mutable signs are Gemini, Virgo, Sagittarius, and Pisces.

We'll keep it at that for now. These elements are a part of the framework, so knowing this would be handy.

Like the signs, planets in Vedic astrology also correspond with the elements. Each planet is associated with one of the elements, giving it unique characteristics and influences - Jupiter is linked to Space, Saturn is associated with Air, Mars is connected to Fire, Mercury is related to Earth and Venus is aligned with Water.

Making sense of the Framework

You now have a grasp on the components of astrology: signs, planets, and houses and how they interact. In astrology, the ideal balance of energies is called "Kalapursha," where everything aligns perfectly—the signs and houses sync up, and planets settle in their ideal signs, creating a potent mix of energy. But this perfect alignment isn't our everyday reality.

We're all works in progress, and our planets don't align perfectly, often finding themselves in unfamiliar territory. Each planet has its comfort zone and unique strengths, learning and the universal arrangement requires them to step out and adapt.

When planets find themselves in houses or signs that don't quite suit them, it's like a pro athlete playing a different sport—they're not at their peak performance because their skills don't match the game, they're in.

Your astrological chart is unique. It's a snapshot of the planets' positions across different signs and houses at your birth. This unique positioning shapes your individual life experiences. Even within a single sign, the energy can vary—the influence starts gentle, peaks in the middle, and eases towards the end. That's why energies within the same sign can be so different.

This diversity within each sign and the planets' varied placements adds depth and uniqueness to everyone's astrological blueprint. By understanding their position and influence, we can gain insights into our life's challenges and comforts, learning more about ourselves in the process.

As we embark on this exploration together, it's important to remember that the arrangement of planets at your birth wasn't something you consciously choose. Whether this setup was a subconscious decision is a topic for another time, but what is crucial here to understand that you were born into a specific arrangement of planets and signs and into a particular culture, surrounded by people and opportunities unique to that environment. Much of our lives are spent interacting with these elements, often without fully grasping their impact on us.

Consider the house you were born in as your first vantage point, the lens through which you began to see the world. This unique perspective shaped your understanding of everything around you. For instance, if your first house is in Cancer, your relationship with your mother and the emotional bonds you formed would be significant. Then, imagine you turn to your left and see in the second house, the sign of Leo is Venus – a water planet, which prefers comfort, might struggle with Leo's fire energy and is fixed by nature. This alignment can influence your perception of Venus-related aspects in your life. You might get restless while sitting idle.

Now, if Saturn were several houses away from your first house, its influence might be less noticeable to you. You wouldn't be as familiar with its energy or effects.

Moreover, each planet has its own perspective and interacts differently with your mind which represented by the Moon. It's no wonder our minds are often filled with a myriad of thoughts and feelings.

The aim of this conversation isn't to overwhelm you but to simplify these complex astrological concepts. It's essential to recognize that your life experience is uniquely yours. No one else can fully understand or feel it as you do.

Your journey through life, influenced by the unique combination of houses, signs, and planets in your astrological chart, shapes a distinct mix of emotions, situations, and perspectives. This personal path offers immense opportunities for reflection and growth.

Understanding your life's framework through astrology is not just about knowledge; it's about aligning yourself with your surroundings to feel complete and empowered. This insight provides a powerful tool and an opportunity for consciously creating your life. When you grasp the intricacies of this 'game' of life, you gain control and get access to the power to shape your existence in the way you desire. Without this understanding, life can feel like mere survival.

It's easy to get caught up in analysing and logically dissecting these astrological influences, but that's not the primary intention here. Nor is it to find fault in your planetary alignments or to judge your experiences as right or wrong. Remember, the universe is inherently perfect and always in harmony, even if this sometimes conflicts with our existing knowledge or beliefs.

The purpose of this book is not to argue over the correctness of different astrological interpretations. Instead, it is to use this knowledge to empower you to handle life's challenges more effectively. The goal is to offer each reader a chance to identify where their power might be misaligned or missing and to provide insights on how to restore it. By understanding your unique astrological makeup, you can navigate life's journey with greater awareness and strength.

As we progress in this book, we'll explore every facet of your being and your unique astrological makeup. We'll not just talk about theories; we'll engage in practical exercises. These exercises are designed to help you observe and feel the influence of astrology in your own life.

If you approach these exercises with intention and authenticity, they can bring profound changes and can possibly transform you. By participating wholeheartedly, you can unlock new dimensions within yourself. This book isn't just about gaining knowledge; it's about you experiencing real breakthroughs in areas of your life where you've felt a lack of power or control.

These exercises are more than simple tasks; they are tools for transformation. They will guide you to a deeper understanding of how the planets, signs, and houses manifest in your life. As you work through them, you would discover insights and paths that were previously hidden.

My promise to you is this: by committing to these exercises and exploring the depths of your astrological blueprint, you'll open doors to personal empowerment and growth. You'll find ways to harness your unique strengths and navigate life with renewed energy and clarity. This journey is about reclaiming your power and creating your life consciously, in alignment with the cosmic forces that shape your existence.

Meditation has opened up profound experiences in my personal journey, including moments of bodylessness. During these meditations, I've encountered a unique state where my mind is active and capable of manifesting thoughts, yet there's a sense of helplessness. In this state, thoughts arise, but there's no ability to change or act upon them. It's a state of complete stillness, devoid of any inertia.

These experiences have led me to a deep appreciation of the physical body. Our bodies are not just vessels; they are incredible blessings, providing us the opportunity to enact change, break old patterns, and create something new and impactful. It's through our physical existence that we can transform thoughts and intentions into tangible actions and realities.

The upcoming chapters of this book are dedicated to leveraging this unique human capability. We will explore ways to disrupt habitual patterns and forge new, empowering paths consciously. This is a privilege exclusive to our human experience – the ability to transform our inner world and, consequently, our external reality.

As we progress, remember that your body is an instrument of change and a catalyst for growth. The exercises and insights provided are tools to help you harness this power. This is our opportunity to make the most of our human potential, to shape our journey consciously, and to create a life that resonates with our most profound truths and aspirations.

How to Engage with This Book for Maximum Benefit

Before we delve deeper, it's essential to define what we mean by 'power.' Commonly, power is defined as the ability to turn your vision into reality, to execute plans with the desired outcomes, and to communicate in a way that your words lead to effective action. However, it's crucial to recognize that sometimes, what seems like power might not be true power. For example, you might be born into wealth or a position of authority, giving you a sense of power derived from your circumstances rather than from within you. This kind of power can be inconsistent and fleeting, often disappearing when those external resources are no longer available. True power is different.

True power is the ability to create action and results regardless of your situation or the resources at hand. It's about having the capability to act and make decisions effectively, no matter the circumstances. This is the kind of power we aim to explore and cultivate in this book.

To truly benefit from this book, I encourage you to start by identifying an area in your life where you feel a lack of power, particularly where you're not taking action or perhaps have even given up. This area, which feels stagnant or hopeless, will be our focus as we apply the laws of the power framework.

As we introduce and delve into each law, we'll directly address these powerless areas in your life. We'll ask tough questions and seek breakthroughs. To facilitate this change, there are some ground rules we need to follow. Let's discuss what these are to ensure you gain the most from this journey and rediscover your inherent power.

In this book, we'll be adopting a learning approach similar to the Vedantic tradition, which encompasses three essential stages: sravana (learning), manana (reflection), and nididhyasana (implementation). This methodology ensures that we not only learn the concepts but also reflect on them deeply and apply them in our lives. It's about connecting meaningfully with what we learn and putting it into action.

To truly benefit from this process and achieve breakthroughs in areas where you feel a lack of power, there are some ground rules that you'll need to follow. These rules are crucial for guiding you through your journey of empowerment. Remember, if you find yourself struggling or not making the progress you desire, it's likely that one of these ground rules needs more attention. These rules are the foundation of your journey through this book. By adhering to them, you set yourself up for meaningful change and empowerment in your life.

Ground Rule 1 - Embrace Authenticity

The first and foremost rule in your journey through this book is to be authentic with yourself. Authenticity is the cornerstone of reclaiming your power. If you're not honest and straightforward with yourself, the insights and exercises in this book won't be effective. Remember, this book is a personal space for growth and reflection, free from external judgments.

The importance of authenticity cannot be overstated. Without it, there's no real path to discovery, and the prospect of recovering your power remains distant. Failing to be authentic means that this book will become just another item in your collection, with no significant impact on your life.

However, if you approach each exercise with sincerity and truthfulness, the value you derive from this book would be immense. I promise you that following the exercises with a commitment to authenticity can transform your life experience. It's not just about learning new concepts; it's about undergoing a profound transformation that can empower you in ways you've never imagined.

Exercise 1: Identifying Your Area of Powerlessness

Now that we've established the importance of authenticity, it's time for you to take the first step in this transformative journey. Your task is to identify an area where you feel a distinct lack of power and have been unable to take action. This could be any domain of your life, whether your career, relationships, finances or any other aspect where you've felt stagnant or powerless.

Grab a pen and paper, or use a digital note-taking method, whichever you prefer. The act of writing it down is a powerful tool in acknowledging and confronting the issue. Write the following sentence, completing it with the specific area where you feel powerless:

'The life area where I lack power is

____

This exercise is crucial. By pinpointing and acknowledging the domain where you feel powerless, you set the foundation for the work we're going to do in this book. It's a critical first step toward understanding and eventually reclaiming your power in this aspect of your life.

Ground Rule 2 - The Power of Reflection

Socrates famously said, 'An unexamined life is not worth living.' This profound statement underscores the importance of self-reflection, a critical component of personal growth and empowerment. In this book, I'll introduce you to a powerful method of self-enquiry that involves having an honest and reflective conversation with yourself.

This method is simple yet profound. You start by asking yourself a question and then authentically answer it in such a way that the answer leads to another question until you reach a more profound understanding or an actionable insight.

Let's apply this method to the area of your life where you've identified a lack of power.

You've already pinpointed where you feel powerless. Now, let's delve deeper into understanding why. The question to ask yourself is, 'Why am I not taking any actions in this life area?' Initially, you might come up with surface-level reasons related to time or circumstances, but it's essential to recognize that these are often just excuses.

As you continue probing, you'll likely reach a deeper layer of truth. Often, the real barrier is a judgment or belief about yourself. It could be thought like 'I'm not capable of achieving X' or 'I'm afraid to face Y.' This self-limiting belief is what is holding you back. Identifying and acknowledging it is crucial because it's the key to unlocking your power in this area. Everything else becomes manageable once you address this core issue.

So, complete the following statement with your honest insight:

'I am not taking action in the life area
____
because I think I _______________________________________
and   I   feel
____ about
the whole situation.'

Write this down. It's a vital step in your journey. Once you have your statement, you're ready to proceed to the next ground rule and further into your path of self-discovery and empowerment.

Ground Rule 3 - Seize the Moment for Reflection and Action

Let's explore the concept of effectively utilizing time and space, especially in challenging moments. To illustrate this, let me share a personal experience. I'm usually punctual but ran late for the office one day. Right below my office building, I encountered a traffic jam caused by someone who had parked their car incorrectly. Frustrated by this disruption to my routine, I felt my sense of power slipping away.

After parking my car a few blocks away and walking back, I found that the incorrectly parked car had moved, and the traffic was back to normal. Reflecting on this incident, I realize there was a golden opportunity to maintain my power, an opportunity that's not present now. It is in the heat of the moment that we truly can grow and harness our power. You can't plan for these moments; how you respond to them as they arise really matters.

Think about applying this in a scenario where you're lacking power. For instance, if you're facing academic challenges and someone doubts your abilities or offers discouraging remarks, that's your moment to reflect. In these moments of confrontation or doubt, the opportunity to grow is most potent.

The inquiry process here isn't about finding direct answers; it's about asking questions that lead to more questions, providing deeper insights about yourself. In management, there's a concept called the 'Five Whys,' where each answer leads to another, more profound question. This method helps you drill down to the issue's core, eventually uncovering actionable insights.

So, when you face moments of weakness or challenge, be fully present. Use these moments for reflection and inquiry. Remember, it's not about finding immediate solutions but understanding the deeper dynamics at play.

Ground Rule 4 - Commit to the Exercises

The exercises provided at the end of each chapter are a crucial part of this journey. These aren't just casual suggestions or optional activities; they are integral to your process of self-discovery and empowerment. Therefore, you must approach these exercises with commitment and diligence.

The actual value of this book lies in actively engaging with these exercises. They are designed to help you apply the concepts you've learned, reflect on your experiences, and initiate meaningful life changes. Skipping these exercises means missing out on the core benefits this book offers.

Remember, the exercises are your tools for transformation. They provide a practical way to implement your learning principles, allowing you to see their impact on your life first hand. By dedicating yourself to completing these exercises, you're taking an active role in your journey towards reclaiming your power and reshaping your life.

So, as you progress through this book, treat the exercises as essential assignments. They are your stepping stones to growth, understanding, and empowerment. No exercises, no value – it's as simple and profound as that.

PART II

The Power Framework

7 Laws at work

Law 1: Law of Correspondence

At the foundation of the Power framework is the Law of Correspondence, a principle that simplifies the understanding of our astrological influences without the need for an astrologer. This law is about recognizing the reflections of our inner energies in the external world.

Take a moment to reflect on your life – your situations, the people you interact with, and the emotions you frequently experience. These external aspects are a direct mirror of the energies inside you. The emotions represented by your astrological signs and planets residing within find expression in your life's circumstances and relationships. This mirroring effect provides a powerful tool for self-awareness and understanding.

Conversely, you can also use your external experiences to gain insights into your internal state. If you notice areas in your life where action is lacking, desired results aren't manifesting, or where you've given up, these are key indicators. They signal a potential mismatch or imbalance in your internal energies.

The essence of the Law of Correspondence is the idea that what's inside is manifested outside, and vice versa. By observing and understanding this correlation, you can start to identify where your power may be diminished and begin the process of reclaiming it. This law encourages you to use your life experiences and body as a mirror, reflecting your inner state and guiding you toward greater self-awareness and empowerment.

Building on the foundational Law of Correspondence, let's dive deeper into the fascinating interplay between the astrological houses and signs and how this relates to our personal journey towards empowerment and self-discovery. The ideal alignment of houses and signs is a state of perfect harmony, a reflection of enlightenment where our external experiences and internal energies are in complete sync. However, this perfect match is more an exception than the norm in our human experience.

We exist in physical bodies precisely because our internal energies and external circumstances are not always perfectly aligned. Our lives are a continuous process of growth and evolution, marked by moments of alignment and misalignment between our inner state and the world around us. This dynamic interplay offers us a unique opportunity to observe, reflect, and adjust as we navigate through life.

For instance, examining your relationship with your mother or your connection to your homeland can shed light on the condition of the Cancer sign within your astrological chart. This reflection can reveal insights into your need for security, belonging, and emotional nurturance. Similarly, exploring how comfortable you are with exploring the unknown, like venturing into dark caves, can reveal your emotional relationship with Scorpio and your capacity to deal with the mysteries of life.

Another aspect to consider is your drive for progress and eagerness to move to the next level. This can illustrate your connection with Aries, highlighting your assertiveness, courage, and initiative. Each sign and house in your astrological chart offer a unique lens to view and understand different facets of your life and personality.

By observing the gaps between your experiences and the ideal state of alignment, you can begin to identify areas where you might be giving away your power or where imbalances in your internal energies might be manifesting especially in your identified area. This process of observation and reflection is not about striving for perfection but embracing the journey of becoming more aligned with our true selves.

In essence, our journey through life, with its challenges and triumphs, serves as a mirror that reflects our internal state. By paying attention to these reflections, we can gain deeper insights into ourselves and take proactive steps toward reclaiming our power and moving closer to a state of harmony and fulfillment.

Exercise: Reflecting on the Impact of Inaction

Embarking on this exercise will illuminate the ripple effects of inactivity or surrender in a specific area of your life. It's designed to help you recognize the breadth of energy being unwittingly sapped by unresolved challenges and the consequent impact on various facets of your existence.

Acknowledging that each segment of our lives is intricately woven together, it becomes clear that overlooking an issue not only depletes our energy but also hampers our efficiency in seemingly unrelated domains. Facing these challenges head-on empowers us to recapture our vitality and enhance our overall quality of life, irrespective of the outcomes.

Through the lens of the Law of Correspondence, this reflective exercise encourages a deep, present engagement with your circumstances. By meticulously examining the repercussions of your actions (or lack thereof), you're invited to a greater understanding and reclamation of your power.

Begin by identifying the specific life area where action has been lacking. Then, methodically outline the other areas of your life affected by this inaction. Structure your reflection as follows:

The areas impacted by my not taking action in my area of ____ **is**

Area 1: ____

Area 2: ____

Area 3: ____

For example, if the focal area is finance, your reflection might look something like this:

The areas impacted by me not taking action in my area of **finance** is:

Area 1: I do not socialize much and meet old friends.

Area 2: I do not indulge in my hobby of painting.

Area 3: Discontent within my family dynamics, particularly affecting my relationship with my wife

Following our exploration of how inaction affects various aspects of life, let's delve deeper to uncover such inaction's emotional and external consequences. This part of the exercise is crucial for recognizing the full scope of how not addressing key issues can permeate your emotional well-being, relationships, and physical health.

Identify Your Top 3 Emotions:

Reflect deeply on the emotions that surface due to the lack of action in an area that matters to you. It's important to articulate these feelings as they reveal the emotional cost of inaction. Write them down as follows:

Emotion 1: _______________________________________

Emotion 2: _______________________________________

Emotion 3: _______________________________________

These emotions could range from feelings of restlessness to irritation or beyond.

Impact on Others:

To draw a complete picture, it is equally important to consider the ripple effect of your inaction on those around you. Often, our challenges don't exist in a vacuum and can affect our presence and interactions with others. Identify how your situation impacts them:

Impact 1: _____________________________________

Impact 2: __________________________________

Impact 3: __________________________________

This might include not being fully present in your relationships or causing concern among loved ones.

7 Spiritual Laws of Power

Physical or Bodily Impact:

Lastly, turn your attention inward to recognize any physical manifestations stemming from this inaction. This can range from a decline in physical health routines to a noticeable drop in your engagement with life's activities.

Impact 1: ____

Impact 2: ____

Impact 3: ____

Acknowledging these impacts is more than an exercise in self-awareness—it's a foundational step toward regaining the energy and vitality currently entangled in unresolved areas of your life. Confronting these truths authentically lays the groundwork for a transformative journey toward a more vibrant, engaged, and empowered existence.

Law 2: The Law of Gender

The second fundamental law in our exploration of the Power framework is the Law of Gender. This law provides a foundational perspective for our work with astrology and personal empowerment.

In the universe, every creation embodies both positive and negative aspects, a duality that is inherent and essential. When we apply this to our astrological framework, it means that each sign, each house, and each planet possesses both negative and positive qualities. It's crucial to understand that this duality is not a flaw – it's a fundamental design of the universe. The existence of the negative is necessary for the positive to be meaningful and vice versa.

According to this law, remaining in power involves emphasizing the positive over the negative. It's about creating a 'throttle' for movement and momentum in your life. By understanding and applying the Law of Gender, we focus on amplifying the positive aspects while gradually reducing the negative influences. This approach generates more momentum and velocity in the areas of life we wish to improve.

This law is universally present, but often, due to a lack of awareness, we fail to exercise conscious control over it. It's a natural human tendency to fall into patterns without realizing the underlying forces at play. By becoming aware of and actively engaging with this law, we can take control of these dynamics. Remember, there's nothing wrong with this inherent duality, or having negative energies is bad; it's an essential part of being human and the universe's design. Our task is to understand and use it to our advantage for personal growth and empowerment.

Exercise: Identifying Positives and Negatives in Your Chosen Area

Having identified the area where you feel a lack of power and understood its impact, it's time to delve deeper. This exercise involves listing the negative and positive aspects of that area. By doing this, we're not jumping into action just yet. Instead, we're developing an awareness of what's working for and against us in this specific domain.

Step 1: List the Negatives

Think about the factors holding you back from taking action in this area. These could be beliefs, circumstances, or external factors that seem to stand in your way. Be honest and detailed in your assessment. For example, you might feel that someone won't listen to you, or you might believe that the goal requires more resources than you currently have. Write down these negative aspects.

Things not in my favour are :-

Negative 1: ____

Negative 2: ____

Negative 3: ____

Step 2: List the Positives

Now, shift your focus to the positives — the aspects in your favour in this area. These could be your skills, supportive relationships, available resources, or any internal or external factor that can help you. Remember, you're not taking action yet; recognize and acknowledge what's on your side.

Things in my favour are :-

Positive 1:

____

Positive 2:

____

Positive 3:

____

This exercise aims to create a balanced view of your current situation. By being aware of both the positive and negative aspects, you can better understand the dynamics at play. This awareness is crucial in preparing to reclaim your power in this area of your life.

Power is staying one step ahead of life… No matter what..!!

Law 3: Law of Completion

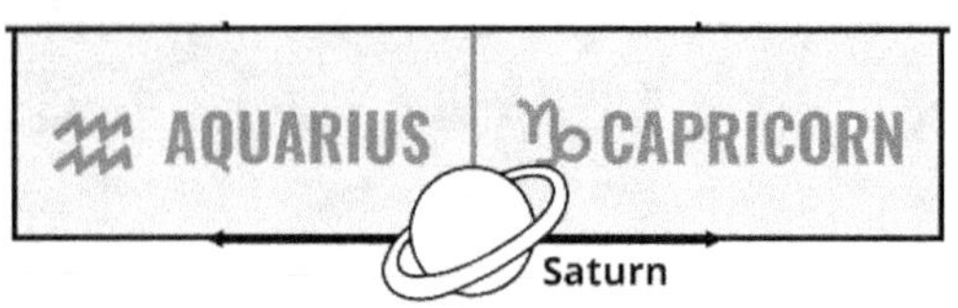

Saturn, a planet of foundational energy, operates through two signs: Aquarius, which carries a positive charge, and Capricorn, which is more negative in nature. Aquarius is an air sign that promotes the completion and elevation of tasks, while Capricorn, an earth sign, tends to ground tasks through fear, holding them back if they are incomplete.

The effectiveness of Saturn's energy lies in its ability to provide a strong foundation. If Saturn's influence is weak in your life, it often manifests as a sense of incompleteness or instability across various areas. This concept applies to every aspect of life but is particularly impactful at the foundational level. Incomplete tasks or unfulfilled promises, like a chair with a broken leg or a car with a flat tire, lack the power to stand or move forward effectively. Saturn uses Capricorn's gravitational pull to keep these incomplete aspects grounded.

Aquarius, on the other hand, is characterized by its straightforwardness, honesty, and adherence to values and ideals. Incompleteness in commitments or expectations leads to emotional baggage, draining your power and presence in the world. Remember, it's not just situations that are incomplete;

it's often a reflection of something within yourself that needs addressing. The law of correspondence applies here.

This principle is vividly illustrated in my personal experience with financial challenges in business. In an attempt to focus solely on financial success, I neglected other areas of life that brought me joy and fulfilment, like exercise, family time, and hobbies. This created a sense of incompleteness and loss of power in those neglected areas, which in turn, affected my performance in business.

Let me take this further. Once, there was a man fervently searching for something under a streetlamp. His focus and determination caught the attention of a passer-by, who decided to stop and see if he could offer some assistance. Together, they scoured the ground, looking for the lost item.

After a few minutes of fruitless searching, the passer-by asked, 'What exactly are we looking for?' The man replied, 'I dropped my keys and can't find them anywhere.' Sympathizing with his plight, the passer-by knelt and joined the search with renewed vigour.

As time passed, however, it became clear that the keys were nowhere to be found in that area. Puzzled, the passer-by inquired, 'Are you sure you dropped your keys here?' The man pointed towards a dark alley a little distance away and said, 'No, I actually dropped them over there.'

Surprised, the passer-by asked, 'Then why are we searching here?' The man looked up with a resigned expression and replied, 'Because it's too dark over there. Here, at least, we have some light.

The story of the man searching for his keys where it's light, rather than where he lost them, humorously mirrors how we often approach our problems. We tend to address what seems accessible or visible, neglecting the real issues that lie in the dark, unnoticed areas of our lives. Engaging with these real issues often requires confronting uncomfortable truths and realities, which Saturn, especially through Capricorn, desires us to do.

To align with the Law of Karma and Saturn's energy, it's essential to consciously work towards resolving areas of incompleteness in our lives. Incompleteness often brings emotions like stress, fear, anxiety, and restlessness – all tools of Capricorn – leading us to apply hard work and effort. By addressing and completing these aspects, you can reclaim your power and see improvements across all areas of your life.

Exploring Saturn's influence in our professional life through Houses 10 and 11 offers another way to understand our career and the rewards it brings. House 10 focuses on our career and how we serve people, suggesting that our fears and challenges at work reflect Saturn's lessons. House 11 shifts the focus to the rewards from our actions, including recognition and achievements. The ease of obtaining these rewards can indicate how well we're aligning with Saturn's principles in our efforts and contributions.

By examining both houses, we gain insights into our professional path and the outcomes of our work.

The relationship between houses and signs isn't this direct and straight forward, yet it's a helpful starting point for exploration.

Exercise: Restoring Power by Completing Tasks and Resolving Incompletions

This exercise is designed to help you reclaim your power by addressing areas of incompletion in your life. It involves three tasks that focus on different aspects of incompletion and the steps you can take to resolve them.

Task 1: Address Shortcuts and Incompletions

List all the shortcuts you've taken or tasks you've left incomplete in your chosen life area. Think about the casual cover-ups you've done to avoid dealing with them. This could be as simple as making a phone call you've been putting off, renewing an important policy, fixing something broken in your home, or any other task you've avoided. To decide what needs to be on this list, pay attention to how each task makes you feel. If the thought of it brings up feelings of irritation, anxiety, or fear, it's a sign that it's draining your power and should be included. Put as many as you can in the format below —

Incomplete Tasks

1. ____

2. ____

3. ____

4. ____

5. ____

6. ____

7. ____

8. ____

9. ____

10. ____

Now, create a plan to finish these tasks. As you finish each item, be present to see the power being restored to you.

Task 2: Fulfil Social Commitments

Reflect on the promises you've made to others but haven't kept and the expectations placed upon you due to your relationships, positions, or agreements.

1. ____

2. ____

3. ____

4. ____

5. ____

Consider how you can fulfil these promises or commitments. It's vital for your empowerment to address these social obligations.

Reach out to people you haven't spoken to in a while, especially if there are unresolved issues or grudges. Clearing these can release a lot of pent-up energy.

Each time you tick off a task from your list, you'll feel a boost in your energy and power. Some tasks seem daunting, and the fear of not succeeding might hold you back. It's completely normal to feel this way; after all, we're all human. However, it's crucial to consider the negative impact of leaving these issues unresolved. Not dealing with them can lead to feelings of anxiety, stress, and unease. Give yourself a week to work through these tasks and notice the positive changes in your life.

If you've managed to check off tasks, well done! Take a moment to appreciate your efforts and achievements. Things might not always go as planned, and that's okay.

If some tasks remain unchecked, that's perfectly fine. Keep the list open, as we'll revisit it. This list will serve as a master checklist, a reference point we'll return to. You may even find yourself coming back to check some more boxes as your read upcoming sections.

Remember to acknowledge both what you've accomplished and what you haven't. We are all perfectly imperfect, and that's absolutely okay. Avoid feeling guilty if something unwanted surfaced during the execution or blaming yourself for uncovering long-buried issues. It's time to address these hidden matters.

Completing tasks will naturally elevate your sense of achievement and bring a feeling of closure. There's something extraordinary about reaching a state of completion.

Also, notice if fear is stopping you from tackling these tasks. This fear indicates Saturn's influence, showing us where we need to grow and strengthen.

As we move further in this journey to next rule, I would take another opportunity to talk about another powerful emotion – Fear. Be present how much fear is stopping you to take actions on these tasks – this is Saturn in play, Saturn in action. Before we move away from this topic, let's pause to explore this powerful emotion that often holds us back: fear.

Its influence can be profound, and understanding how to confront and manage fear is crucial for gaining back power. An old European folktale beautifully illustrates the nature of fear and how to deal with it. Let me share this story with you.

Once, an adventurous traveller arrived at a city gripped by fear and terror. The city's inhabitants lived in constant fear of a giant monster that lurked on the outskirts. From a distance, the monster appeared enormous, towering over the landscape like a mountain. Its mere presence cast a shadow of fear across the city, with people terrified that it might one day enter their homes.

Although the traveller had faced many dangers, he had never encountered a creature of such colossal size. He decided to confront the monster, promising the frightened citizens that he would deal with the threat. With a mix of fear and determination, he set out towards the monstrous figure.

As he left the city limits, the traveller noticed something surprising. The monster, which had seemed so gigantic from afar, was not as large up close – maybe only ten times his size. Though still intimidated, he continued to approach, taking one step at a time.

With each step, an astonishing thing happened: the monster began to shrink. The closer the traveller got, the smaller the monster became. By the time he was just a few feet away, the creature was only the same size as him. And as he took one more step, the monster diminished to the size of a pebble.

The traveller picked up the tiny monster, holding it to eye level, and asked, 'Who are you?' The monster replied, 'I am your fear. I appear large and daunting from a distance, but all it takes to conquer me is to move towards me, one step at a time.'

This fable sets the stage for our next two rules: Vision and Action. It teaches us that action without vision can lead us astray, while vision without action remains unfulfilled. Both elements require power to be effective. Like the traveller in the story, confronting our fears with steady, deliberate steps can transform something seemingly insurmountable into something manageable. As we move forward, remember the lesson of the fable: facing our fears, step by step, reduces their fear grip over us and clears the path towards achieving our vision and goals.

Knowing where to go is powerful but knowing where you are stuck is even more powerful..!!

Law 4 – The Power of Purpose

Let's explore Jupiter's realm, a key area in our journey of harnessing power. Jupiter, a symbol of expansion, rules over Sagittarius and Pisces. It embodies the energy of growth, utilizing Sagittarius's positive attributes for propulsion and Pisces's negative traits as brakes.

Sagittarius is all about focus and high performance. Picture the centaur with four legs for stability and a bow and arrow for precise targeting. The clarity of goals is critical here – clearly defined objectives form a significant part of achieving any aim. To expand and grow 10X, you need to set goals 10X larger. The wisdom in this approach is echoed in the ancient epic Mahabharata, where Arjuna, a master archer, is asked to target a fish's eye. His focused vision, seeing nothing but his goal, is a vital lesson in success.

This idea is reinforced in modern self-help classics like "Think and Grow Rich" and Earl Nightingale's "The Strangest Secret." Both emphasize the significance of having big, ambitious goals. These goals are what fuel your enthusiasm each day. They are the charges that ignite your actions and align them with creation.

Your beliefs, represented by Jupiter, are the foundation upon which you stand and act. They drive you, consciously or unconsciously. Defining your beliefs gives you direction and space for expansion. In the grand scheme of things, Jupiter's love for creation and expansion supports your growth through these goals. Its physical representation as the largest planet in our solar system symbolizes its expansive nature.

In a more tangible sense, Jupiter manifests as mentors or teachers in House 10 who can help expand your horizons. True expansion often requires guidance from others. Without external input, a person alone cannot become 'two' or 'eleven'. Those who've achieved your aspirations can guide you. This is especially true if you know exactly what you want and truly want it. When you're authentic about your goals, mentors will come to you on their own. Remember, what you feel inside will show on the outside.

Earl Nightingale highlights the most common shortfall in personal power – the absence of substantial goals. Many are caught up in life's routine, never pausing to consider their true direction. Setting a goal is challenging; it confronts the comfort of the status quo. Yet, once set, there's no turning back. The book you're reading is a testament to the power of goal-setting – it's a product of my vision transformed into reality.

Your goal is your guiding star, keeping you on track amid life's distractions. When you feel lost, refocus on your goal. If something doesn't align with your goal, it's probably not worth your time and energy.

However, the challenge lies in the energy of Pisces, which teaches detachment from specific outcomes. Often, we're so fixated on a particular result or path that we fail to see other possibilities. For instance, I held onto a failing business out of attachment, draining my energy and causing frustration. It was only when I released this attachment that I regained my freedom and power. Letting go of specific outcomes, especially when they don't align with our larger goals, is crucial in maintaining our power.

In conclusion, Jupiter's energy teaches us the importance of goal-setting and the wisdom of detachment. Embrace expansive thinking, guided by clear goals and an open mind to various pathways to achieve them. This approach will not only keep you aligned with your purpose but also ensure you remain adaptable and resilient in your journey.

Imagine pursuing your goals as navigating through a maze. You start with a clear vision of your goal - visible, attainable, and something you earnestly desire. As you progress towards it, you're filled with purpose and determination. But then, inevitably, you encounter a wall - a seemingly insurmountable obstacle.

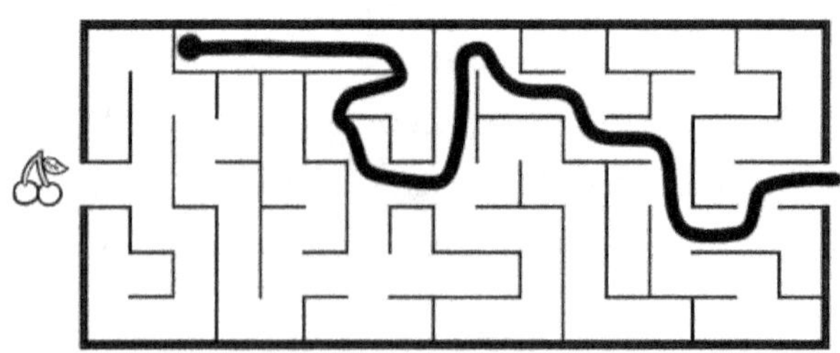

At this point, it's all too easy to become fixated on this barrier. You've come so far, invested so much, that this wall becomes your entire world. You might find yourself pushing against it with all your might, hoping it'll budge. Or, perhaps you set up camp right there, praying for a miracle or, in a state of resignation, leaving your goal unachieved, your journey incomplete. This spot, right against the wall, is where your power is at its lowest.

In careers, relationships, and various life endeavours, these walls appear. And here's where the crux of the journey lies: if you're genuinely committed to the result, you must detach from the notion that there's only one way to achieve it. The maze of life is riddled with walls, and the key to navigating it is the willingness to backtrack, to retrace your steps, and to seek a new path when faced with an impasse.

This flexibility requires immense power and courage. Many spend their entire lives stuck at their first wall, unable to turn around and try a different route. Pisces teaches us this valuable lesson - if it's not serving your ultimate goal, release your attachment to it. Our fixation on achieving results in a specific way often makes the idea of turning back, of trying something new, unbearably painful.

The essence of this approach is a commitment to the end result, not to the means or the specific path you initially chose. Pisces helps us let go of what's unnecessary for our growth. Clinging to these redundant elements only drains our power.

When you learn to stay focused and committed to your goal while being open to different paths and outcomes, you've essentially mastered the maze. Your growth, then, is not just about reaching the end but also about the journey itself, which is an invaluable part of the process.

While simple in theory, this concept can only be truly understood through experience. It's about aligning with Life's natural ebb and flow, being adaptable yet focused, and understanding that sometimes the best way forward is a step back to find a new route or just to go along with Life's flow. It's a dance with the universe, where commitment to your goal and openness to change go hand in hand.

Task 1: Set a Clear and Measurable Goal

When it comes to setting goals, clarity and specificity are your best allies. It's not just about stating what you want to achieve but also defining it in a quantifiable way. For instance, if your focus is on improving your relationships, a goal could be to limit arguments to just one per week. Setting a clear goal provides a benchmark to strive towards and evaluate progress against. If your ambition is financial stability or growth, set a concrete figure you aim to reach by a specific date, whether saving $10,000 by year-end or cutting down unnecessary expenses by 30% within six months.

The adage that only 3% of people have written goals seems like an interesting comparison; I do not know it for a fact yet it carries a profound implication: those with clearly defined and documented objectives are often the ones who end up leading or influencing others. The rest, the 97%, tend to fall into routines dictated by the paths created by those with clear goals.

To gain control in your chosen area of life, it's crucial to have a clear goal defined.

My Goal in my life area of ______________ **is**

____

____

____

____

____

Task 2: Select a Mentor

Find a mentor, guru, or coach who has achieved what you aspire to. This should be someone whose accomplishments and methods resonate with you.

Please do thorough research before, but once you establish a connection with them, commit fully to their teachings without doubt or suspicion. Trust the process and their guidance, setting aside your preconceptions and logic. Just like you need someone else to help you lift your body because you can't do it alone, growing and improving work the same way; if someone has already gone through what you're facing, their experiences will navigate your journey, which is very supportive and critical.

Task 3: Develop an Empowering Belief System

Create a set of affirmations that encourage expansion and align with your goals.

You can choose your affirmations in any format, but when you first read them, these affirmations should challenge and stretch your current belief system.

It's okay if they seem silly or unrealistic or don't make sense initially. It's great if they do! You would find many affirmations online, so pick one that feels right for you. They could read something like this if your area of work is wealth.

"I am a magnet for prosperity, and wealth naturally flows to me from multiple sources."
"Every day, in every way, my income increases by leaps and bounds."
"I am financially free, with abundance flowing into my life effortlessly."

"My actions create constant prosperity, and I am aligned with the energy of abundance."

"Wealth is a positive expression of divine energy, and I always have more than enough."

"My mind is a powerful catalyst for financial success and innovation."

"I embrace new avenues of income and welcome the financial security it brings."

"My wealth is a reflection of my inner belief in abundance, and I attract success every day."

"I am deserving of prosperity, and I release all resistance to wealth now."

Write these affirmations daily and pay attention to any internal resistance they provoke. This practice will help you identify and move beyond limiting beliefs, allowing for greater growth and expansion.

Write down your affirmations here: -

Task 4: Explore New Actions

Examine why you're stuck in your chosen area or repeating ineffective actions. Think about new, different actions to bring about positive change.

Commit to these new approaches, ensuring they're innovative and not just slight variations of your past efforts. Stay open-minded and unattached to previous methods or expected outcomes. The key is to remain flexible and adaptable, ready to explore uncharted paths.

Write them down: -

____

____

____

____

____

____

____

____

____

____

____

____

____

Your Action is a direct measure your power

Law 5 - The Law of Action

In the realm of astrology, we now turn our focus to Mars and its significant impact under the Law of Action. Mars, particularly in the sign of Aries, is about the drive to ascend, conquer new heights, and push boundaries. Aries is where Mars thrives, fueled by the desire for action and progress. The more you invest Marsian energy into your endeavours, the higher you can potentially rise.

However, Mars also brings with it a challenge – the uncertainty of outcomes. This uncertainty can be a significant deterrent to action. When you're engaged in creating or achieving something, there's often no clear indication of when or how the desired results will manifest. This ambiguity can be disheartening. It's not uncommon to see others achieving success with apparent ease, which can lead to frustration and self-doubt. You might find yourself questioning your efforts, especially when they go unrecognized, leading to hesitation or even cessation of action.

Scorpio, another domain of Mars, adds a layer of darkness and uncertainty, often stemming from past experiences and energy accumulations. Actions taken under Scorpio's influence can feel like shots in the dark, with outcomes less predictable than one might hope. This can lead to a feeling of being lost, like stopping just short of finding gold because you're unsure if you're on the right track. The mystery and unpredictability inherent in Scorpio's energy can significantly affect your sense of power and direction.

Given the importance of results in motivating action, examining our relationship with outcomes becomes essential. How we handle the absence of immediate results can either empower us or drain our energy. Understanding this dynamic helps cultivate the power to act despite uncertainties and continue striving even when the path ahead isn't clear.

Geeta sums it up in a very powerful way in Chapter 2, Verse 47

कर्मण्येवाधिकारस्ते मा फलेषु कदाचन।

मा कर्मफलहेतुर्भूर्मा ते सङ्गोऽस्त्वकर्मणि॥ 47 ॥

<u>BG 2.47</u>: *You have the right to perform your duties but are not entitled to the fruits of your actions. Do not consider yourself the cause of your results, nor be attached.*

This principle is vital in understanding how the desire for results can hinder our ability to move forward and take effective action in the present. Results are often influenced by myriad unknown factors, including past karma, making it hard to predict when you will reach your peak.

This principle is vital in understanding how the desire for results can hinder our ability to move forward and take effective action in the present. Results are often influenced by myriad unknown factors, including past karma, making it hard to predict when you will reach your peak. You might be just an inch away from striking gold, or it may still require a lot of digging, you do not know.

The idea of working without a direct focus on the outcomes might seem counterintuitive, but it's essential to view the entire picture. With clear goals and a solid action plan, you act diligently. Being complete in your actions and giving your best ensures that the results, whether as expected or not, do not diminish your power.

If the outcomes don't align with your expectations, the key is to quickly reassess and explore other options that lead to your goal without losing power in the process. This approach doesn't imply a reduction in effort; it's about maintaining focus and energy regardless of immediate results.

For instance, consider a cricket batsman aiming for a six. He takes his shot with all his might and focus, and he gives the best he has, but once the ball is in play, the result is out of his hands. If the ball doesn't reach the boundary, dwelling on this missed opportunity can sap his energy. Instead, the quicker he refocuses on the next ball, the better his chances of achieving the team's target.

The Bhagavad Gita, in its profound wisdom, offers insights into how to find power in action. This ancient scripture presents concepts as relevant today as they were thousands of years ago.

कर्मण्यकर्म यः पश्येदकर्मणि च कर्म यः ।

स बुद्धिमान्मनुष्येषु स युक्तः कृत्स्नकर्मकृत् ॥ *18*॥

<u>Bg 4.18:</u> Those who see action in inaction and inaction in action are truly wise amongst humans. Although performing all kinds of actions, they are yogis and masters of all their actions.

This verse invites us to a deeper understanding of our actions and their nature. It encourages us to perceive the subtleties of action and inaction, a concept that transcends mere physical activity. This wisdom is not just to be understood intellectually but experienced at the very core of our being.

Consider moments in life when you engage in activities that you truly enjoy, like cooking, painting, or being in nature. In these moments, time seems irrelevant, and you become one with your activity. There is a sense of profound connection and power in these experiences. This is where you and your work are not separate entities but a unified force. Such moments reveal the true nature of your relationship with your actions.

To delve into this concept, reflect on instances where you've been completely absorbed in an activity, like playing chess and being so engrossed in the game that nothing else exists. However, when a sudden turn of events in the game challenges you, you become distinctly aware of yourself. This shift from being 'nothing' to suddenly becoming 'something,' offers a powerful insight into your self-perception and how you define yourself in action.

The Bhagavad Gita's teaching becomes even more poignant when we consider its context - a dialogue between Lord Krishna and Arjuna in the midst of a battlefield. It is in this setting of imminent action, where Arjuna faces a moral and existential crisis, that Krishna imparts the wisdom of 'action in inaction.'

This teaching is about recognizing moments when our self-assessment intrudes on our actions. The moment we start judging or defining ourselves, especially in challenging situations, we shift into a survival mode. This mode is inherently powerless and impacts the results of our actions. The more we get caught up in self-judgment, the more we distance ourselves from the essence of our actions and the power they hold.

The Bhagavad Gita's message here is profound. It asks us to explore and understand our relationship with action and inaction, to discover our true selves in the midst of our activities, and to learn how to act without the constraints of self-judgment. This exploration is essential in understanding the dynamics of power in action.

When encountering moments of inaction, it's an opportune time to actively reflect and understand what's hindering your ability to act. These moments are not mere pauses; they are gateways to introspection and self-realization. It's in these periods of inaction that you can most effectively identify and confront the aspects of yourself that are blocking your path to action.

This process is about recognizing the *'you'* that stands in the way of *'your'* actions. It's about understanding that sometimes, the biggest obstacles to our progress are internal — our perspectives, habits, or rigid ways of thinking.

The key to overcoming this inaction lies in identifying just one element within yourself that, if let go, can catalyze action. This could be anything from a stubborn attitude to an unyielding method of operation. Once you pinpoint this one aspect and authentically let it go, you will notice an immediate surge in your power.

Here's an everyday example: imagine you're at work, and your boss wants to tackle a project one way, but you're set on doing it another way because it's how you've always done it. Now, consider the first thing you can drop to make this project move forward. It might be your ego or your need to be right. Let go of that one thing in conversation with yourself, and watch how it changes things. Keep letting go, one thing at a time, until the job is done. This moment is your chance to grow stronger and more capable. Once the task is complete, the moment passes, so seize this chance to expand your power.

Initially, this practice might require effort and conscious attention, but over time, as you become more adept at self-reflection, this process of letting go will become more natural and intuitive.

This concept is beautifully symbolized in Indian mythology through the worship of Kirtimukha, often depicted at temple gates. The legend of Kirtimukha begins with its creation by Lord Shiva, who empowered it to vanquish a demon. When the demon surrendered, Shiva commanded Kirtimukha to consume itself. The act of self-consumption, surrendering and overcoming one's own barriers, was seen as a sign of ultimate power. Thus, Kirtimukha became a revered symbol, representing the power of self-transformation and the importance of conquering one's own limitations before seeking the divine.

The extent to which our identity, or self-assessment, interferes with our work is a crucial aspect to consider in the Law of Action. This self-assessment dictates how we perceive and approach our tasks. The same work that might feel burdensome to one person could bring immense joy to another. This difference in perception is often rooted in the identity we associate with ourselves and the task.

The key here is to understand the effort needed to complete a challenging task is directly proportional to the extent of our identity that we infuse into it. If a task feels arduous and draining, it's likely because we are too entangled in our own self-assessment related to the task. This could manifest as a dislike for the work, a belief that it doesn't align with our skills or a feeling that it's beneath us. To gain ease, velocity, and power in action, it's essential to let go of these parts of our identity that are creating resistance.

This approach ties back to the concept of action in inaction, as mentioned in the Bhagavad Gita. When we successfully detach our identity and self-assessment from the task at hand, we reach a state where we become one with the action. In this state, the action unfolds effortlessly, without the need for forced effort from our end. It's a harmonious blend where the doer and the deed merge, leading to a seamless flow of action.

Practically, this means approaching your work with a mindset where your personal judgments, prejudices, and ego do not dictate how you engage with it. It's about focusing on the task with pure intention, free from the constraints of your self-imposed identity. This purity of action ensures that the work is not only done efficiently and effectively, propelling you forward in the area of your life you're focusing on, but also self-liberating, powerful medium.

The profound experience of becoming one with the task at hand is something that cannot be fully conveyed through words; it must be experienced personally. This state, where you are completely immersed in the act of creation, is where the true power of action lies. When you merge with your tasks, moving beyond the need to assess and judge the results, you open yourself to a realm of heightened power and expansion.

I have personally navigated this process while writing this book. There were moments when I was dissatisfied with how the content was shaping up, leading me to delay the work, waiting for a sense of perceived perfection. However, each time I let go of these assessments and focused solely on taking action, I made progress. It is through continuously dropping these self-judgments that the book eventually came to fruition.

This approach aligns with what many creators and innovators known as the '90% failing rule' — the understanding that 90% of new endeavours might fail, but it's the 10% that succeed is what matters. The key is not to focus on the failure or success rate but to fully integrate oneself with the task, deriving power, growth, and learning from the process itself. This integration ensures that your entire being is powered and aligned with your goals.

Additionally, the reluctance to act often stems from a fear of failure. As discussed under the Law of Completion, fear is a domain of Saturn. In Indian culture, this concept is acknowledged through the joint worship of Lord Saturn and Lord Hanuman, symbolizing the balance between facing our karmas (Saturn) and the need for action and strength (Hanuman). After seeking Saturn's blessings for the power to deal with our karmas, it's equally important to invoke Hanuman's energy for the courage and strength to act, ensuring we don't falter under the weight of our karmic responsibilities.

This synergy of action and strength, coupled with the understanding of our karmic journey, forms a vital aspect of overcoming fear and moving forward with purpose and power.

Taking action can really change your life, even if you're not feeling great or you're worried about things you've done in the past. If you act honestly and do the right thing, you'll move past those old troubles. Starting something new might feel weird or scary, and you might get nervous or feel a bit sick. That's okay and happens to everyone. The important thing is to keep going with your actions, and after a while, they'll start to feel normal and become a regular part of your life.

The concept of action in our lives extends far beyond the mere completion of tasks; it is fundamentally about learning and growth. When you achieve a state of oneness with the task you're engaged in, a profound transformation occurs - the task and you become indistinguishable. This unity is not just a philosophical concept; it is the very essence of why we exist in physical form. It's about leveraging our bodily experiences for spiritual and personal growth.

In this context, the material outcomes of our actions, while essential in our earthly journey, are transient. They remain behind when we depart from this physical world. However, the growth and empowerment we achieve at the level of our being are enduring. They continue with us as a part of our spiritual essence, represented in Vedic astrology as Ketu memory. This accumulated growth and power from our actions become the foundation for our soul's journey to its next phase.

Therefore, each action we undertake should be viewed through the lens of personal and spiritual growth. Approaching tasks with this mindset transforms them into opportunities for profound development. This approach ensures that our actions are not just mechanically performed but are deeply integrated with our purpose and spiritual progression.

Exercise

This exercise aims to deepen your mastery over the Law of Action and integrate the teachings from Saturn (the Law of Completion) and Jupiter (expansion and detachment from outcomes).

Start by revisiting the list of incomplete tasks from the Saturn exercise. Reflect on what aspects of your being, such as certain traits or habits, prevent you from completing these tasks. It could be anything from a need to control every detail to a tendency to procrastinate. Choose one primary trait that you feel is a major hindrance and make a conscious decision to let it go. Approach the task anew, this time with a mindset of surrender, focusing solely on the act of doing rather than how it is being done.

Write it down like this:

I am willing to give up my ________________________________ to ensure that I generate power in my actions in my life area of

____

After completing the task, take a moment to observe the outcome. Remember the lesson from Jupiter about detachment from results. Try to understand what the completion of this task and the process of letting go of a hindering trait teaches you. This is not just about finishing a task; it's an exercise in self-improvement and empowerment.

Repeat this process, each time identifying and letting go of another trait that hinders your action. This iterative method will help you move closer to effortless action, where tasks are completed with ease and without the burden of self-imposed barriers.

Additionally, identify tasks within your area of focus that you find unpleasant or burdensome. As you engage in these tasks, pay close attention to how you show up. Are there feelings of resentment, lack of interest, or impatience? Pinpoint what internal resistance, such as a particular mindset or expectation, you can let go of to make these tasks more manageable. Once you've identified this resistance, approach the tasks again, having released it. Notice the difference in your experience of the task and the level of empowerment you feel.

Law 6 : The Power of Choice

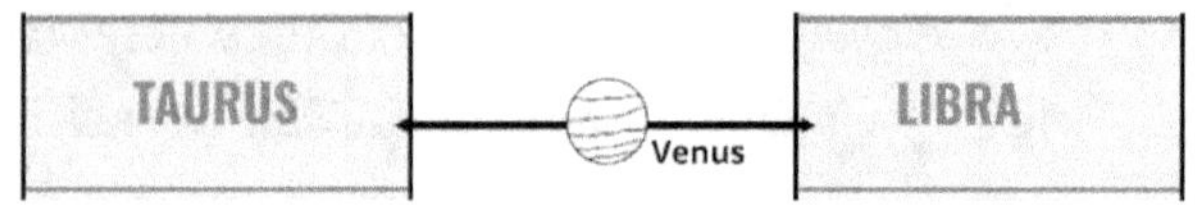

We have entered the domain of Venus, a planet that significantly influences our human experience in a good way. Venus is synonymous with comfort, luxury, food, art, and essentially all the finer things in life that many aspire to have. It governs two signs, Taurus and Libra. Taurus carries a negative charge, while Libra is on the positive side. In our journey, we'll lean more towards the positive aspects of Libra within the framework, aiming to harness more power for impactful results.

Understanding the nature and role of Venus is crucial, particularly in the context of the power framework. Venus, with its comforting attributes, can sometimes act as a force that encourages rest and relaxation. This is reminiscent of the classic tale of the hare and the tortoise. In this story, the hare, confident in its lead, decides to take a break just before the finish line, illustrating how Venus can sometimes induce a state of rest or complacency. This aspect of Venus is universal, a natural phenomenon allowing those more persistent, like the tortoise, to catch up.

Observing the impact of Venus in real life, it's not uncommon to see individuals who reach a certain level of comfort in their careers and life and then lose the initial drive and zeal for further growth and expansion that was present at the beginning. This shift in attitude and motivation, influenced by the Venusian energy, plays a crucial role in discussing power and how it manifests in our lives.

Taurus represents the material possessions and luxuries in our lives, things we naturally desire to enjoy. It's essential to recognize that there is nothing inherently wrong and that the world, in its essence, maintains a balance and harmony in this space. However, it's crucial to examine our lives authentically and assess whether we are becoming complacent or resting on the laurels of our comforts. This complacency can manifest when there's no longer a perceived need to pursue further goals because the power and security of wealth and luxury seem sufficient.

I recall a phase during my corporate tenure when I found myself in this comfortable space, so I understand how subtly this can occur. Venus, in this context, shouldn't be seen in a negative light. It plays a vital role in our lives, with money and luxury serving as central forces for existence. The point here is to be mindful and vigilant. Are you easing off on your ambitions and goals, perhaps subconsciously, due to the comforts and luxuries you've attained? This self-awareness is critical in understanding how Venus influences our drive and motivation.

Venus symbolizes our comfort zone, an area often characterized by a lack of significant results. Within this comfort zone, there's an underlying push and restlessness, a subtle demand from life for more, yet it's challenging to pinpoint the exact source of discontent. This comfort can inadvertently act as a brake, slowing or even halting our actions and pursuits. When we stop taking action, we stop seeking the power needed to create and innovate. In its extreme form, remaining in the comfort zone for too long can lead to lethargy and laziness, a state where growth and progress are hindered.

In the realm of emotions, Venus represents our habits. Often, we become constrained by these habits, consistently preferring to do things in familiar ways because it feels comfortable. This habitual approach to life means we tend to follow patterns that we're used to rather than exploring new or challenging methods.

Venus, a water sign, occupies a significant part of our personality, much like water, constituting about seventy percent of our body. Our habits, deeply influenced by Venus, play a critical role in shaping who we are.

These habits dictate our actions, often leaving us with little perceived choice. We find ourselves repeating actions and behaviours simply because that's how we've always done them. This repetitive cycle is so ingrained in our nature that trying new ways of doing things can feel unfamiliar and uncomfortable.

The influence of our habits is so profound that they can shape our future, a fact that astrologers often utilize. By observing the nature of planets, particularly Venus, an astrologer can anticipate our future actions based on the assumption that we will continue to follow our established habits. Deeply rooted in our past, these habits tend to repeat themselves with only minor variations. If we lack conscious awareness and presence in our daily lives, we inadvertently carry these past habits into our future. This cyclical nature of habits and their impact on our life trajectory is not overly complex but is a fundamental aspect of human behaviour.

Every part of our body holds a memory, a concept that has been scientifically validated and understood by sages for thousands of years. Venus plays a crucial role in this aspect of human life, acting as a continuous loop that is challenging to break. Its function is to carry forward experiences and tendencies from the past into the future. Consequently, the outcomes of our actions often become predictable, rooted in past patterns and habits. This cycle gives the impression that our lives are predestined, akin to a drop of water flowing along a river's current, with little choice or control over its path. Venus, in this context, symbolizes the inertia of life's trajectory, driven by the momentum of past actions and habits.

Reflect on this analogy: Imagine a boat adrift in water. Without any effort, it moves with the current, and if there are tides, its movement is even more pronounced. This scenario represents life's flow, where various events unfold simply because you find yourself in the stream – influenced by the family or country or culture you were born into, and the opportunities that naturally arise from these circumstances. These events, both successes and failures, often feel predestined, occurring as a result of your placement in the flow of life rather than your conscious choices or actions.

When life's current carries you effortlessly, it's often enjoyable, but only as long as it aligns with your desires and goals. The real challenge arises when you're swept away in a direction contrary to your aspirations. In these moments, you might feel powerless, unable to influence or change the course of events. This sensation is akin to being alive without truly living — days may pass without colour or excitement, lacking the spark of inspiration that comes from actively steering your own journey.

You might label these experiences destiny, luck, or the natural order of things. They seem to occur spontaneously, without your direct influence or control. This feeling of being carried along by forces greater than yourself is a common stage in life. Yet, it raises an important question: how can one generate personal power in such circumstances where control seems elusive or non-existent?

No action you take sitting on the boat will help because the current is strong. One thing that can help is discovering for yourself that you are not much powerful enough to change the flow of water just by sitting in the boat. What options do we have here to stay in power?

Sitting on the boat, you may realize that any action you take seems futile against the strong current. This leads to the understanding that you lack the power to change the water's flow from your current position. So, how can you maintain your power in this scenario?

The current in this analogy represents our habits and established ways of doing things. This habitual pattern places us in a compulsive state. Remember, in the context of Venus, these habits and comfort zones dictate our actions. We're often trapped in doing things the same way, expecting different outcomes. It's essential, therefore, to scrutinize these habits and compulsions before proceeding with any new actions.

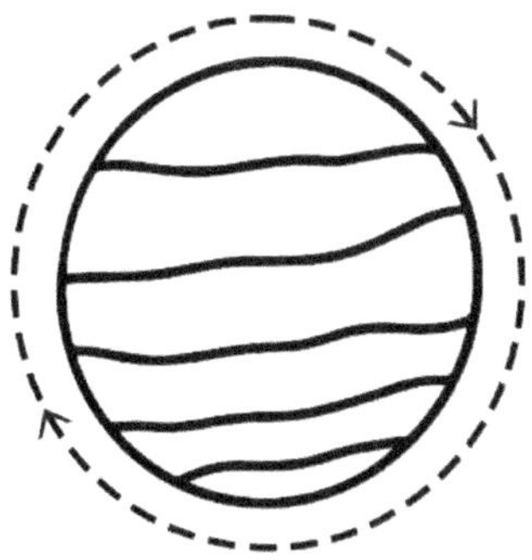

Any action you do out of compulsion will not give you any different results. Actions taken out of compulsion rarely lead to different outcomes. If you're on a boat, drifting along with the same current and flow of the water. No matter how much effort you put into steering the boat, it will still follow the water's path.

To effectively address this, consider if there's a way to significantly influence the water's flow—perhaps by rowing. Working directly with the flow of water may create an opportunity for a change in direction and results. Although it might not immediately take you to your desired destination, it opens the door to new possibilities. Persistently rowing and altering the water's current can gradually align you with the direction you wish to head.

Stepping out of your comfort zone unleashes a tremendous amount of power from nature, helping you navigate new situations and balance their outcomes. The intention isn't to rush you into hasty decisions but to open a window for introspection—reflecting on the extent of your compulsion towards habits and understanding their impact on your life.

Libra offers a unique power exclusive to humans—the freedom to choose. All decisions allow you to make choices. If your decisions or choices are based on past, Venus has a strong influence. However, if your decision is made solely based on present moment, Venus holds minimal influence. When you make choices that are unburdened by the past, new possibilities are sure to emerge.

The concept of making unbiased choices is challenging to grasp and can only be truly understood through experience. When you make choices not influenced by your past experiences, they are untainted and can lead to different outcomes in the future. Repeating the same actions while expecting new results is futile. Libra empowers you to make choices that are not dictated by your past, thereby freeing them from bias, weight, and limitations. Choosing independently from past influences is liberating and powerful. Each time you break free from the past's grip, a fresh surge of power is unleashed within you.

Libra possesses the strength to think with balance and make potent choices and decisions.

When you authentically start to look at your life and reflect on it, there emerges power and choice to make some changes to it to get new results. You may not initially get the results *you* want, and I am asserting you would not in the first time. It would require changes at the being level, but you would discover a new and powerful you every time you choose and make a decision free from the past.

When you begin to examine your life and reflect upon it genuinely, you unlock the power to make choices that can bring about new outcomes. Initially, these changes might yield different results than you desire, and that's expected. Significant changes often require profound shifts at the core of your being. Each time you make a decision not influenced by your past, not only do you untangle yourself, but you uncover a stronger, more empowered version of yourself. This process helps you transcend being a mere puppet of circumstances, embodying the true essence of power.

A unique human attribute is the ability to choose. You have the freedom to continue in your current powerless state or to explore new possibilities that lead you to different results. The decision is always in your hands. You can opt to address a situation head-on or choose to linger in resentment. Every choice you make shapes your journey and defines your relationship with power.

When you default to the routine responses to life's daily demands, simply going through the motions, you inevitably surrender your power and drift along life's current — what's often referred to as "the grit of life." Therefore, it's crucial to make your choices deliberately and thoughtfully. By doing so, you can break free from the past's hold — the influence of Venus — and chart your own course, one driven by conscious decision-making rather than habitual reactions, and that is power.

Power, in the context of Venus's influence, is about breaking free from habitual patterns and exploring new approaches. The upcoming exercise focuses on identifying unfinished tasks and re-evaluating how they are approached. The goal is to move away from your comfort zone and habitual methods, thereby challenging the stagnation that Venus can sometimes induce.

Exercise

Reflect on tasks in your area of life that remain unfinished. These could be personal or professional goals, projects, or even relationship improvements. Acknowledge that your current methods, influenced by past habits and comfort, lack the power to complete these tasks effectively. This isn't a fault in your actions but a natural tendency influenced by Venus.

Think of an entirely new approach to one of your unfinished tasks. This should be something you haven't tried before. For example, if you've been tackling a project alone, consider collaborating with others for fresh perspectives. Focus on a method that challenges your comfort zone. If you typically avoid confrontation, address an issue directly. Choose an innovative or creative solution that differs from your usual routine. If you're dealing with a personal goal, such as fitness, try a new exercise regime or sport instead of your usual workout.

Define three new actions you can do that you have not done before in your area of life that can change the flow of actions and directly impact the outcome.

____

____

____

____

____

By executing these new actions, you're not just attempting to complete tasks; you're actively shifting the flow of your actions. This change can directly impact outcomes and help you reclaim your power, moving you away from the predestined path set by past habits. Remember, it's about breaking the cycle of comfort and predictability that Venus often brings and embracing the power of choice and change.

Power exists in language .. and so does lack of it.

Law 7 – The Power to Create

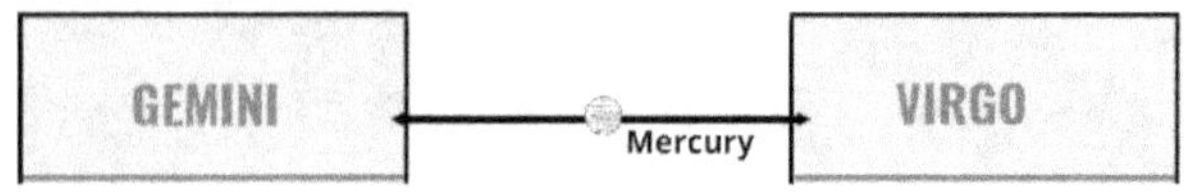

In our exploration of the power framework, we now approach the domain of Mercury. Despite being the smallest planet in our solar system, Mercury holds significant influence. It orbits close to the Sun, both in our celestial neighbourhood and in astrological significance. Mercury, mainly composed of iron, symbolizes the hard, unyielding truths of life. It epitomizes objectivity, leaving little or no room for subjective emotions and feelings. Mercury represents the tangible and quantifiable aspects of existence.

Consider aspects of life like your height, weight, the balance in your bank account, or the distance to your office. These are all measurable entities grounded in reality. Mercury's role is to cut through the emotional overlays we often attach to such facts, allowing us to see things as they truly are, not just as we perceive or believe them to be. This ability to discern the bare facts is a powerful tool.

As humans, we often become deeply attached to meanings, interpretations, and narratives, which can diminish our control and power over situations. Mercury's domain encompasses all that is quantifiable and concrete in our world - distance, time, and physical attributes. Everything beyond these measurable aspects is essentially a construct of the mind. In fact, when these mental constructs strip us of our power, they become counterproductive to creation.

Mercury's influence extends to Gemini and Virgo, each sign manifesting its power directly and differently. Gemini, in particular, is characterized by duality. It exists within the contrasts of big and small, good and bad, demons and angels. In essence, every aspect of creation is defined in comparison to something else. This dichotomy inevitably leads to the formation of opinions, biases, and prejudices, along with the associated emotional and mental baggage.

Operating within the confines of these dualities can be limiting and can diminish our power. When we constantly compare and contrast, our actions and creations are bound by these parameters, restricting our ability to think and act freely. Understanding the role of Mercury in these signs can help us navigate these limitations and find ways to exercise our power more effectively, free from the restrictive framework of dualistic thinking.

Understanding the significance of language in the context of power in the domain of duality is crucial. Both power and powerlessness are also in duality and intricately linked to how we use language. Let's delve into how.

Language is the medium through which we express our thoughts, feelings, and experiences. It is the tool we use to communicate with ourselves and others, whether through spoken words, written text, sign language, or any other form of expression. The essence of language originates within us.

To grasp the impact of language on our sense of power, it's essential to introspect and consider how much of our communication is influenced by the dualities we perceive - categorizations like good and bad, big and small. Imagine the potential shift in the effectiveness and power of our conversations if we removed these dualistic comparisons. Our communication often suffers from biases and prejudices that stem from such comparisons. For instance, when we compare ourselves to others, it can lead to feelings of inferiority or superiority, which in turn distorts the truth and reality of the situation.

Language extends far beyond mere communication; it encompasses every aspect of our feelings and self-expression. The true power lies in listening, not just in the act of speaking. By paying close attention to how we express ourselves, both internally and externally, we uncover valuable insights into our constraints and limitations. The barriers we perceive are often constructed within the confines of language itself, having no tangible basis in reality. Recognizing that these barriers are our own linguistic creations offers us the power to dismantle them. This awareness is profoundly empowering. Listening attentively to our inner voice, something many of us neglect or actively suppress, can lead to a deeper understanding of ourselves. Often, we overlook or silence this inner dialogue, but it continuously communicates with us, offering insights and guidance. By tuning in to this internal conversation, we can uncover what truly holds us back, realizing that much of it exists solely within the realm of language. This shift towards active listening can illuminate our internal landscape, revealing pathways to overcome self-imposed limitations and fostering a more profound connection with our authentic selves.

The actual loss of power doesn't come from external situations, people, or circumstances but rather from the meanings we attach to them and how we express these meanings through language. Imagine observing a colleague's larger home or a neighbor's luxury car and the internal narrative it triggers. If this narrative weakens you, it signals an opportunity to become more aware and not surrender your power to these external comparisons. The key lies in your response and the interpretations you choose to make. By relinquishing the constructed meanings that disempower you, you reclaim your power. This process underscores the significance of perspective and the transformative potential of viewing challenges not as sources of loss but as opportunities for growth and self-awareness.

Thresholds also exist in Language

Thresholds exist in language, a concept that becomes evident when we closely examine the moments leading to a perceived loss of power.

Let me share an experience to illuminate the idea: On the last day of the year, I was driving to the office early in the morning. Given the holiday season, the roads were unusually empty, a rare sight in the bustling city. Approaching a small intersection, I stopped at the traffic signal, facing a countdown of 160 seconds. This extensive wait at such a minor crossroad struck me as odd, especially when no other vehicle was in sight, abiding by the red light alongside me.

As the counter dwindled to 20 seconds, an intriguing pattern of human behavior unfolded. Despite the earlier opportunity to cross without delay, it was within these final 20 seconds that drivers chose to stop as if the shortened wait now fell within an acceptable threshold of patience.

Observing that about 8 out of 10 cars willingly halted for this brief period highlighted a profound insight into how we define our limits, not through physical constraints but through the boundaries we establish in language.

This morning's observation serves as a metaphor for
the limitations we impose on ourselves, often dictated by the language of our thoughts and the arbitrary thresholds we accept as our reality. Increasing our power and expanding beyond these self-imposed confines necessitates pushing against these thresholds, challenging the barriers erected by language, and

redefining the "not for me" moments into opportunities for growth and transformation.

The first step in regaining power is recognizing the existence of a threshold and being consciously aware that you've surrendered power to it. It's important to acknowledge that while physical constraints and hurdles exist, the power we attribute to them is primarily constructed in language. This difference in language is why some individuals appear to navigate the same challenges with greater ease than others.

They employ a different narrative, a distinct linguistic approach that doesn't empower the hurdle similarly, allowing them to transcend these barriers more smoothly. Wrapping up, remember that calling things negative or bad can drain your energy. So, choose your words wisely to keep your power.

To further explore the profound impact language has on our power and how we navigate life's realities, let's engage in an exercise designed to deepen our understanding.

Exercise

In this final part of our journey through the book, let's closely examine a moment when you felt powerless. Think back to that specific incident and narrate in detail what occurred. Share your feelings about it as if it's happening right now. Make the story as vivid and lively as possible. This is your chance to be complete with that experience, so give it your full attention. Don't rush ahead; focus on this exercise first. This step is crucial; skipping it means missing out on a significant opportunity to understand how power is lost in everyday life.

Let me share an example here, narrating a day from Tina's life when she was feeling low and disempowered:

As I was leaving the office, I decided to call Jacob, my boyfriend, to see how his day was going. But as soon as he answered the phone, I could tell something was off. He seemed distant and preoccupied, and didn't offer any explanation when I asked him what was wrong. I couldn't help but feel hurt and confused, and I couldn't shake the feeling that something was wrong in our relationship.

Feeling down, I decided to go for a walk to clear my head. As I was walking, I couldn't help but think about all the things that had gone wrong that day. I felt like my dog had been lost, my boyfriend was not paying attention to me and I was not feeling good about myself. I felt like my life was falling apart, and I couldn't understand why.

As I walked, I came across a poor lady and started comparing my life with hers. I don't know why, but looking at her, I felt a little better for myself. I realized that even though I had a lot of problems in my life, I was still blessed with many things. I felt grateful for what I had and thanked God for all the things he had offered me.

Feeling a little better, I walked back to my home. As I walked, I realized that even though my day had been bad, it wasn't the end of the world. I knew that things would get better and that I would make it through this tough time.

I got home, and I did not feel like speaking to Jacob, I felt too hurt and upset. I decided to take some time for myself and relax. I felt a sense of calm and peace, knowing that everything would be alright. I knew that I would make it through this tough time, and that things would get better.

The next day, I woke up feeling refreshed and ready to take on the day. I knew that things wouldn't always be easy, but I was determined to make the best of it. I decided to focus on the positive things in my life and to be grateful for all the blessings that I had. I knew that with a positive attitude and determination, I could overcome any obstacle and make my day a good one.

Now narrate your event here in a similar way, where you felt loss of power.

____

____

____

____

____

____

____

____

____

____

____

____

____

____

____

____

____

____

____

____

Once you have narrated the event, the day you dealt with less power, let us find where the loss of power was in the whole event. We would do something very interesting. Let us strike out what was not real in the incident. When I say real, let's bring out just the physicality of things. Anything that could be described in time, distance, volume, area, dimension, or time for its exactness would stay, and the rest would be eliminated. Let me do that in the sample above.

As I was leaving the office, I decided to call Jasob, my boyfriend, ~~*to see how his day was going.*~~ *But as soon as he answered the phone,* ~~*I could tell something was off. He seemed distant and preoccupied, and didn't offer any explanation when I asked him what was wrong. I couldn't help but feel hurt and confused, and I couldn't shake the feeling that something was wrong in our relationship.*~~

~~*Feeling down,*~~ *I decided to go for a walk to clear my head.* ~~*As I was walking, I couldn't help but think about all the things that had gone wrong that day. I felt like my dog had been lost, my boyfriend was not paying attention to me and I was not feeling good about myself. I felt like my life was falling apart, and I couldn't understand why.*~~

As I walked, I came across a poor lady ~~*and started comparing my life with hers. I don't know why, but looking at her, I felt a little better for myself. I realized that even though I had a lot of problems in my life, I was still*~~

~~*blessed with many things. I felt grateful for what I had and thanked God for all the things he had offered me.*~~

~~*Feeling a little better,*~~ *I walked back to my home. As I walked,* ~~*I realized that even though my day had been bad, it wasn't the end of the world. I knew that things would get better and that I would make it through this tough time.*~~

~~*I got home, and I did not feel like speaking to Jasob, I felt too hurt and upset. I decided to take some time for myself and relax. I felt a sense of calm and peace, knowing that everything would be alright. I knew that I would make it through this tough time, and that things would get better.*~~

The next day, I woke up ~~*feeling refreshed and ready to take on the day. I knew that things wouldn't always be easy, but I was determined to make the best of it. I decided to focus on the positive things in my life and to be grateful for all the blessings that I had. I knew that with a positive attitude and determination, I could overcome any obstacle and make my day a good one*~~

Now, if this was played as a video recording, someone would describe it as –

Tina woke up in the morning and spoke to Jacob. She looked a little upset, though. She went for a walk, saw an old lady, and returned. In the morning, she looked a little relaxed.

Once you've done this exercise for an event where you felt loss of power and crossed the emotions, consider the significant role language plays in coloring our experiences with meaning. It's not those emotions are inherently good or bad—they indeed add vibrancy to life. However, it's crucial to recognize that during moments of perceived weakness or powerlessness, it's often the meanings we attach to events through language that deplete our sense of power, not the actual events themselves.

Now if Jacob was to describe this event, it could be something like –

"Tina called me in the morning, I was busy with some office work and she as usual tried to dominate. She did sound upset and also did not call me at night"

When we distill situations to their essence, removing the layer of personal interpretation, what remains is the raw reality—facts and circumstances we can address directly without the additional weight of our subjective meanings. Gemini, ruled by Mercury, emphasizes the power of language and presents us with the chance to harness power consciously.

Recognizing that any loss of power is a construct of our making in language offers a unique opportunity to redefine our narrative. By choosing to alter or abandon disempowering interpretations in favor of empowering ones, we reclaim our agency and the ability to generate power in any given moment.

Virgo and its association with the sixth house, encompassing competition adversaries, sickness, and diseases, represent significant challenges that can drain our energy and power. However, an effective strategy for overcoming these challenges lies in our response to them.

By choosing not to be affected by adversities and confronting competition with fairness, we can not only enhance our strength but also secure a more powerful position. Adopting a fair approach enables us to embrace greater risks boldly, generating substantial power to lead and excel. It's essential to recognize that the obstacles we face are often constructed and perpetuated through our language and perceptions. To reclaim our power, it becomes necessary to alter the narrative we associate with these challenges. Changing how we speak about and perceive our adversities allows us to assess and amplify our power, turning potential setbacks into opportunities for growth and empowerment.

Exercise:

Engage in a conversation you've been avoiding. Approach it with an open mind and the intention to understand and be understood.

Deliberately place yourself in situations outside your comfort zone, especially those involving interaction with individuals you find irritating. Listen actively, seeking to find value and perspective in their words.

Initiate discussions regarding tasks or projects that remain incomplete within your chosen area of focus. Be mindful of both your language and the language of others during these conversations. Observe how shifts in dialogue can unveil new possibilities and insights.

This is the final set of exercises, so give your best effort.

Moving Forward

As we conclude our journey together through the pages of this book, I sincerely hope you've found value and insight in its teachings. This exploration might have been challenging if you've actively participated in the exercises or pondered the concepts presented. My deepest wish is for you to have cultivated a profound understanding of the unseen forces shaping our lives and, more importantly, that you've embarked on actions that have led to tangible, significant, and impactful results.

Having navigated the intricate dance of planets, signs, and houses, you now stand with a perspective expanded, as if viewing life from ten feet above. This newfound vantage point gives you comprehensive insight into life's myriad obstacles and challenges. By applying the knowledge you've acquired, you've gained not just insights but also powerful tools to address these challenges head-on. This astrological voyage has also deepened your understanding of how your personal energy is distributed and its impact on your daily experiences. Moreover, this book aims to illuminate the dynamic path of personal growth, highlighting how attuning to external influences can steer you toward a life that's not only more empowered but also deeply fulfilling.

It is essential to understand a few things to align powerfully with life and to stay in power, and this understanding has the potential to keep you in a powerful space. Everyone possesses the same amount of energy distributed among the planets, ensuring the sum total is always complete. At any phase or situation, if you feel deprived of power, it's essential to remember that the interplay of planets may create a perception of power loss. However, being consciously present and aware is the key teaching of astrological science.

Recall that ancient wisdom serves a profound purpose: to unveil life's insights and act as a beacon, guiding us toward deeper self-understanding and harmonious existence with the cosmic forces surrounding us. Amidst the hustle of daily life, it's all too easy to forget our higher calling and overlook the subtle energies that mold our reality. Yet, the essence of these spiritual laws urges us to see beyond the mundane to discover the intricate threads that interlace us with the universe's vast tapestry. This invitation to peer beneath the surface not only enriches our journey but aligns us more closely with the universal rhythms that animate our being.

Reflect deeply on the following summary, as it offers a valuable perspective for introspection. Consider the dynamics of your life as either a linear path or perhaps as a pyramid structure. From your inception, there exists a parallel energy flow that moves from the pinnacle to the base and back again. Anchoring yourself on the sturdy support of Saturn lays a solid foundation, energizing your core forces and setting the stage for Jupiter to enhance your creative abilities. This progression kindles the fire within, influencing your emotions and expression and culminating in tangible outcomes within Mercury's domain. If results seem intangible, methodically examining each segment can reveal underlying discrepancies. Results can be intimidating, akin to report cards or balance scorecards, challenging even the most courageous. The essential insight here is to recognize that the outcomes under Mercury's influence are a cumulative effect of all elements below it. Embracing results, identifying corrective measures, and diligently applying yourself to improvement encapsulates the continual growth cycle.

Introspection is invariably beneficial in all areas, let's take an example by examining the dynamics of relationships. By starting at Saturn and advancing towards Mercury, you can uncover potential blockages. Consider whether Saturn's realm instills fears that prevent you from making the initial move. Does Jupiter's influence expose an absence of quantifiable goals in your relationships? Might you be fixating on a singular outcome, overlooking the diverse avenues available for fulfilling your desires? Are you actively employing Mars' energies to take decisive action, or are you finding too much comfort within Venus' domain? This upward analytical model sheds light on the reasons behind your stagnation, offering precise directions for proactive measures.

This journey extends far beyond theoretical musings; it harbours tangible benefits. Pinpointing gaps in various aspects of your life can herald a transformative phase, paving the way toward empowerment and growth. Intriguingly, there exists a concurrent and overlapping path within spirituality known as chakra awakening, deemed one of the most profound journeys a person can embark on. This process delves deep into the spiritual realm, aligning seamlessly with these seven laws and consciously priming you for a transformative spiritual awakening.

The concept of transformation is a fascinating exploration of energy metamorphosing so profoundly that its original form becomes unrecognizable. This process is emblematic of true transformation, a journey where the end state is so distinct from its inception that it leaves no hint of its past. Imagine the transformation of water into ice or a seed into a towering tree. It's a process so complete that one cannot fathom the original state evolving into its final form. Each step towards this transformation is crucial, supported by the appropriate environment and care. This mirrors the astrological journey from Saturn's air release through Mars' fiery fire shaping and beyond. Just as a seed, given the right conditions, grows into a tree that stands in stark contrast to its simple origins, so too does every phase of personal growth contribute to a transformative journey that renders the new form vastly different from its humble beginnings.

This book isn't just a guide; it's a tool for ongoing discovery. By diving into its lessons, you can spark big changes and grow in the parts of your life you want to improve. It gives you the power to choose what you want to focus on and start afresh. The first step might be challenging, but as it begins to click with you, you'll find other areas of your life and work falling into place more smoothly. Returning to these lessons will give you new insights and ways to tackle different parts of your life. Every time you read it, you get a chance to grow and deepen your understanding of how the stars and planets influence your journey. Remember, learning about yourself and becoming more powerful is an ongoing journey, and this book is here to help you every step of the way to reach your highest potential.

Your body is your most powerful tool, so make the most of it. Through learning Theta Healing, I realized how eagerly our souls wait to enter our bodies and start making changes. Many feel stuck because they've lost the ability to take action. So, use this opportunity, go full on and make the most of it. This book is my way of showing you a bit of the incredible journey that's possible for you.

For more insights and tools to support your journey, visit powerframework.com. I'm constantly exploring these topics, and my upcoming book, "The Power to Create," will delve into the intricate ways your mind (symbolized by the moon) shapes your subjective reality and how the power of the Sun can be used to manifest positive outcomes and new possibilities. Additionally, we're developing a personalized report feature on thepowerframework.com, where you can input your birth details and receive a "Power Report." This report will detail the positions and strengths of your planets, aiming to empower you with a deeper comprehension of this science's foundational intentions. So, make sure to stay tuned and subscribe.

Thank you for embarking on this spiritual journey with me. It's a privilege to accompany you. Let's keep in touch and continue to awaken to the cosmic rhythm. Until our paths cross again, may you navigate your journey illuminated by wisdom and boundless creative energy. Stay empowered and inspired. Wishing you peace, blessings and a lot of power as you move forward.